SUPREME AUTHORITY

By the same author:

COMMENTARY ON THE GOSPEL OF LUKE

SUPREME AUTHORITY

The authority of the Lord, His apostles and the New Testament

J. Norval Geldenhuys, B.A., B.D., Th.M.

(Author of "Commentary on the Gospel of Luke" and former Elsie Ballot scholar to Cambridge and Princeton.)

Foreword by
PROF. NED B. STONEHOUSE

WIPF & STOCK · Eugene, Oregon

Wipf and Stock Publishers
199 W 8th Ave, Suite 3
Eugene, OR 97401

Supreme Authority
The Authority of the Lord, His Apostles and the New Testament
By Geldenhuys, J. Norval
ISBN 13: 978-1-55635-768-8
ISBN 10: 1-55635-768-0
Publication date 12/10/2007
Previously published by Wm. B. Eerdmans, 1953

Dedicated to my three sons
DEO, NORVAL *and* ARJEN

FOREWORD

To the non-theologian, as well as to the Biblical scholar, the theme of this book is of profound practical moment. For in treating *The Supreme Authority* in terms of the witness of the New Testament and of the faith of the early Church, the author confronts the reader most basically with the subject of the Lordship of Jesus Christ. This is no merely scholastic question. When the sovereignty of Jesus is acknowledged in word and deed, nothing short of full religious commitment and genuine worship is involved. And the man of faith knows that his life and destiny are at stake in this relationship to Christ.

Today there appears indeed to be an ecumenical concert of voices confessing Jesus as Lord. If it is to be valid and meaningful, however, that acknowledgement surely may not become an equivocal formula or an empty refrain. To be genuine and fruitful, our understanding of the Lordship of Christ must conform to His disclosure in His Word of the nature of His legitimate demands upon us. There is involved, therefore, the Christological question—who Jesus really was and is—but also the question how He mediated His Lordship in history—what authority the apostles and the New Testament are to be recognized as possessing for faith and life. Especially in a time when the Christian proclamation of Jesus as Lord is being interpreted as essentially mythological—and thus as not in verity a Lordship which has come to a once-for-all concrete expression in history—it is a matter of urgency to face these questions. Only thus can one be certain that the sovereignty of Jesus Christ has not become a mere symbol of what may ultimately turn out to be really the autonomy of the human spirit.

This treatise will be welcomed as a fresh and interesting contribution to the study of the authority of the New Testament. It is indeed not an exhaustive work on the subject. Only certain leading factors and aspects of that history come under review and discussion. And the broader question of the relationship of the authority of Christ and of the New Testament to the historic acknowledgement of the Old Testament as Holy Scripture is only touched upon. Nevertheless, we encounter here a valuable and impressive survey of evidence which bears upon such central questions as the authority of Christ, the historical mediation of that authority to His apostles, and the manner in which, by Christ's authority and with His sanction, the authority of the apostles came to expression in their writings.

Norval Geldenhuys, though a minister in the Dutch Reformed Church of South Africa, has become so well and favourably known in the English-speaking world that he needs no personal introduction or commendation here. The cordial reception which his *Commentary on the Gospel of Luke* has received will assure this book a sympathetic hearing. May it serve particularly to arrest attention anew upon the pervasiveness and consistency with which, according to all the Christian records, the Lordship of Jesus Christ was taught and recognized, and upon the decisive significance of this fact for our evaluation of the New Testament.

N. B. STONEHOUSE

Professor of New Testament,
Westminster Theological Seminary,
Philadelphia.

CONTENTS

	PAGE
INTRODUCTION	13
DEFINITION OF THE TERM "AUTHORITY"	15

(A) THE AUTHORITY OF THE LORD IN THE NEW
    TESTAMENT AND THE EARLY CHURCH ... 17

    I. THE AUTHORITY OF THE LORD AS REVEALED IN THE GOSPELS AND ACTS ... 18

    II. THE AUTHORITY OF THE LORD AS PROCLAIMED IN THE EPISTLES AND REVELATION ... 31

    III. THE AUTHORITY OF THE LORD AS BELIEVED IN AND ACCEPTED BY THE EARLY CHURCH ... 38

SPECIAL NOTE: THE SIGNIFICANCE OF THE FACT OF THE AUTHORITY OF JESUS ... 43

(B) THE AUTHORITY OF THE APOSTLES IN THE
    NEW TESTAMENT AND THE EARLY CHURCH ... 45

    I. THE LORD HIMSELF CALLED, EQUIPPED AND SENT FORTH THE APOSTLES ... 46

    II. THE APOSTLES THEMSELVES CLAIMED TO POSSESS AND EXERCISED AUTHORITY ... 65

    III. THE AUTHORITY OF THE APOSTLES WAS ACKNOWLEDGED IN THE EARLY CHURCH ... 85

(C) THE NEW TESTAMENT FORMED AND CLOTHED
    WITH THE AUTHORITY OF THE LORD AND OF
    HIS APOSTLES ... 99

(D) CONCLUSION ... 119

BIBLIOGRAPHY ... 123

ALPHABETICAL INDEX ... 127

INTRODUCTION

THE AUTHORITY of Jesus and of His apostles was of the most basic importance for the beginning and development of Christianity. This may sound like a truism. But it is a lamentable truth that in contemporary New Testament theology very little appreciation is shown of the fact of the Lord's authority in the New Testament and in the Early Church. And we feel convinced that this neglect is the cause of much of the confusion that, after a whole century of discussion, still reigns almost supreme in so many modern theories concerning the history of primitive Christianity and of the formation of the New Testament. Only a vital realization of the supreme fact of the authority of the Lord can enable us to see the history of the beginning of the Christian Church and of the formation of the New Testament in the right perspective. Second only to this is the importance of realizing what authority His apostles possessed. The subject with which we deal in this book is therefore of the utmost significance.

The longer we studied this subject the clearer it became that the only way in which we could hope to do any justice to it would be to let our sources, the New Testament and the other Early Church documents, speak for themselves as far as possible. We shall therefore try to follow a positive method of presentation and only in a secondary way enter into a discussion of the various divergent theories of men like Harnack, Enslin, Bousset, Manson and many others who try to escape acceptance or full acceptance of the New Testament and Early Christian presentation of the authority of the Lord and of His apostles.

DEFINITION OF THE TERM "AUTHORITY"

THE NEW TESTAMENT Greek word for "authority" is ἐξουσία. Foerster[1] shows how in the κοινη Greek it was used of "vön einer höheren Norm oder Instanz gegebene Möglichkeit und damit das Recht, etwas zu tun, das Recht über etwas" (the power granted by a higher criterion or instance, and along with it the right to do something, the right over something) and also comes to mean "power and authority", "permission" and "freedom" to act. It must therefore be distinguished from δύναμις, which means simply "power" in the sense of "der innewohnenden Möglichkeit zum Handeln"; i.e. "the indwelling ability to act".

ἐξουσία could, apart from what we have already mentioned, be used also in other senses which are, however, not of importance here for our discussion. Of greater significance is the fact that the New Testament usage of ἐξουσία is, according to Foerster, influenced by the rabbinical רְשׁוּת. This word points to the right of disposal, and so also "das Besitzrecht über etwas, die Vollmacht oder Beauftragung, das Recht oder die Freiheit, etwas zu tun . . . und wird so auch die Bezeichnung der absoluten, monarchischen Macht Gottes"[2] (the right of possessing something, the full authority or commission, the right or the liberty to do something . . . and so also becomes the description of the absolute, sovereign power of God).

According to B. Davidson[3] the Aramaic word רְשָׁא (which also might have influenced the New Testament usage of ἐξουσία) means "to be able" and "to have permission". And the Hebrew

---

[1] "ἐξουσία", *Theologisches Wörterbuch zum Neuen Testament*, ed. by G. Kittel, Stuttgart, 1935, ii, pp. 559 ff.
[2] *ibid.*
[3] *The Analytical Hebrew and Chaldee Lexicon*.

word יָרַשׁ (from which רְשָׁא and רְשׁוּת are probably derived) means "to inherit", "to possess" and "to dispose".

In the Septuagint ἐξουσία is used to translate the Hebrew מֶמְשָׁלָה, which means "dominion" or "rule". In Daniel it is used also to translate the Aramaic שָׁלְטָן, which means "power" and "authority".

In view of this rich background for its use, it is clear that ἐξουσία is a very comprehensive term and excellently suited to express the idea of an all-inclusive authority, in the sense of the freedom and the power to command and to enforce obedience, and to have possession of, and rule and dominion over.

(A) The Authority of the Lord in the New Testament and the Early Church.

We have divided this first part of our discussion into the following three main divisions:

  I. The authority of the Lord *as revealed* in the Gospel and Acts.
 II. The authority of the Lord *as proclaimed* in the Epistles and Revelation.
III. The authority of the Lord *as believed in and accepted by* the Early Church.

I

THE AUTHORITY OF THE LORD AS REVEALED IN THE GOSPELS AND ACTS

THROUGHOUT the Gospels and Acts our Lord is revealed to us as the Son of God clothed with supreme authority. Already in Matthew i. 23 the Old Testament words "they shall call his name Immanuel[1] (which is, being interpreted, 'God with us')" are applied to the child that is to be born. And of this same child the angel announces to Mary: "He shall be great, and shall be called the Son of the Most High: and the Lord God shall give unto him the throne of his father David: and he shall reign over the house of Jacob for ever; and of his kingdom there shall be no end" (Luke i. 33 f.). A little later the angel states that He "shall be called holy, the Son of God" (i. 35). And after the birth of the Child an angel announces to the shepherds: "there is born to you this day in the city of David a Saviour, which is Christ the Lord" (Luke ii. 10).

In no more explicit way could the supreme authority of the Bethlehem Child have been announced than in these angelic annunciations—He will be the Son of the Most High, the appointed King who will reign for ever, and the Lord ($\dot{o}$ $\varkappa\acute{v}\varrho\iota o\varsigma$).[2]

Gifted with prophetic insight, the greatest of the prophets, John the Baptist, about thirty years later reiterated the angelic announcements of the authority of Jesus, for "he preached, saying, There cometh after me he that is mightier than I, the latchet of whose shoes I am not worthy to stoop down and unloose. I baptized you with water; but he shall baptize you with the Holy Ghost" (Mark i. 7, 8).

---

[1] This term primarily points to the gracious, redeeming presence of God. But it also implies that He has the authority to impart grace and work redemption.
[2] Cf. our discussion of the meaning of this title, *infra*.

SUPREME AUTHORITY

The climax in the annunciations is, however, reached when God the Father Himself in the voice from heaven announced at the baptism of Jesus: "Thou art my beloved Son, in thee I am well pleased" (Mark i. 11), and again at the Transfiguration: "This is my beloved Son: hear ye him" (Mark ix. 7).

Gustav Dalman[1] proves that the expression "the beloved Son" (ὁ υἱὸς ὁ ἀγαπητός) means exactly the same as the expression of John iii. 16: "the only-begotten son" (ὁ υἱὸς ὁ μονογενής). He then declares: "The position of the only (or 'the beloved') son is, in these cases as in Psalm ii, regarded as a lawful status which confers a right to claim the entire household property. In the case of the Son of God the reference can only be to the sovereignty as would be exercised not by a Jewish emperor but by a divine sovereign."

Accordingly by these two announcements, made through the heavenly voice of God the Father at two of the most critical stages in the ministry of our Lord, the Almighty finally and unequivocally proclaimed for all time that Jesus as His beloved Son is indeed clothed with supreme, divine ἐξουσία. And it is significant that in the announcement at the Transfiguration God, through the voice from heaven, after having said "This is My beloved Son", gave the explicit command: "Hear ye Him!"

What our Lord Himself taught

From the very beginning of His ministry our Lord, in complete harmony with the announcements made concerning His authority, Himself declared and taught that He possessed supreme and absolute authority.

Although He never explicitly applied to Himself the title "Son of God", He nevertheless consistently made it clear that He was not merely "a" but "*the* Son of God".

Thus, for instance, He never spoke of God as His and His

---

[1] *The Words of Jesus: Considered in the Light of Post-Biblical Jewish Writings and the Aramaic language*, authorized English version by D. M. Kay, T. and T. Clark, Edinburgh, 1909, p. 201.

disciples' Father, but spoke of "My Father" and of "Your Father", making a clear distinction between His natural and eternal Sonship and the (derived) sonship of the disciples (cf. Mark xii. 1-12; John xx. 17). Jesus separates Himself completely from all others as belonging not to their number but to God, His Father, alone. And that He looked upon His unique Sonship as entitling Him to the throne of God, to absolute authority, is clearly shown in many of His declarations—e.g. Matthew xi. 27: "All things have been delivered unto me by my Father", and above all in His declaration after His Resurrection: "All authority[1] [ἐξουσία] hath been given unto me in heaven and on earth" (Matt. xxviii. 18). Remembering again the rich and comprehensive content of the word ἐξουσία used here in Matthew xxviii. 18 we see that our Lord claims that to Him is given the right, the freedom and the power to demand and enforce obedience, to have unreserved possession of, and rule and dominion over, all and everything in heaven and on earth.

But not only at these great epochs did our Lord claim to possess absolute, divine authority. He made this claim throughout His ministry. He claimed that only He possessed the authority to teach the truth and to reveal God: "All things have been delivered unto me of my Father: and no one knoweth the Son, save the Father; neither doth any know the Father, save the Son, and he to whomsoever the Son willeth to reveal him" (Matt. xi. 27). And in John xiv. 6 He said: "I am the way, and the truth, and the life: no one cometh unto the Father, but by me!", thus claiming that only He possesses the authority to lead men to God. In the first words of the high priestly prayer (John xvii. 2) our Lord declared

---

[1] This proves the truth of Foerster's words: "Eine wichtige Rolle spielt ἐξουσία zur Deutung von Werk und Person Jesu. Es bezeichnet die ihm von Gott gegebene Vollmacht zum Handeln. Ist er der Sohn, so ist auch die ihm gegebene Vollmacht nicht als beschränkte Beauftragung zu denken, sondern als Verwaltung in freier Willenseinheit mit dem Vater zu verstehen" (An important part is played by ἐξουσία in interpreting the work and personality of Jesus. It means the full authority to act, granted Him by God. If He is the Son, then also the full authority granted Him by God is not to be thought of as a limited commission, but must be understood to mean stewardship in free unity of will with the Father (*Theol. Wörterbuch zum N.T.*, ed. by G. Kittel, Stuttgart, 1935, ii, p. 572).

the same fact: "Father, the hour is come; glorify thy Son, that the Son may glorify thee; even as thou gavest him authority [ἐξουσία] over all flesh, that whatsoever thou hast given him, to them he should give eternal life."

Having this authority, it is natural that Jesus claimed also all authority over the kingdom and the Church as is evidenced, for example, in His words to Peter: "Upon this rock I will build my church; and the gates of Hades shall not prevail against it. I will give unto thee the keys of the kingdom of heaven." Also in the following words does He claim supreme authority regarding the kingdom by declaring: "Not every one that saith unto me, Lord, shall enter into the kingdom of heaven, . . . many will say to me in that day, Lord, Lord, did we not prophesy by thy name, and by thy name cast out demons, and by thy name do many mighty works? And then will I profess unto them, I never knew you: depart from me, ye that work iniquity" (Matt. vii. 21 ff.). In Matthew xxv. 31–46 our Lord explicitly declares that at the Consummation He will sit as King on the throne of His glory and judge who is to inherit the kingdom and who is to be sent away into eternal punishment (cf. also John v. 27). And the remarkable thing is that He declares that all men in that day will be judged according to their attitude towards Him. So He places Himself in the very centre of everything as the One possessing supreme authority even over the eternal destinies of men. Only because He is the Son of God, one with the Father and the Spirit, could He and, as the Gospels show, did He claim all this in such a natural but uncompromising way.

Even when He stood accused before the Sanhedrin, humanly speaking conquered and defeated, He made the same astounding claim of possessing absolute authority by declaring: "Henceforth ye shall see the Son of Man sitting at the right hand of power" (Matt. xxvi. 64).

His authority revealed in practice

Jesus, however, did not merely claim to possess authority, but also exercised His ἐξουσία throughout His ministry in word and deed.

He spoke and taught with authority and revealed that He came as the Fulfiller of the Old Testament revelation. He did not come to destroy but to fulfil the law and the prophets (Matt. v. 17). Nevertheless He did two things that implied that He asserted a new and supreme authority. Firstly, He repudiated the scribes' interpretation of the Torah (Matt. xxiii. 13–26) and, secondly, He declared that even some of the Mosaic laws were of temporary and imperfect character and must be replaced or reinterpreted by His own more adequate teaching. "Ye have heard that it was said by them of old time, Thou shalt not commit adultery: but I say unto you, That whosoever looketh on a woman to lust after her hath committed adultery with her already in his heart. . . . Ye have heard that it hath been said, An eye for an eye, and a tooth for a tooth: but I say unto you, That ye resist not evil: but whosoever shall smite thee on thy right cheek, turn to him the other also" (Matt. v. 27, 28 and 38, 39). "In doing this He was really fulfilling a line of thought which permeates the entire Old Testament. All its writers disclaim finality and look forward to a fuller revelation of the mind of God in a day of Jehovah or a new covenant or a Messiah. Jesus Christ regarded these expectations as being realized in Himself, and claimed to complete and fulfil the development which had run through the Old Testament. As such He claims finality in His teaching of the will of God, and absolute authority in the realm of religion and morals."[1]

The very way in which Jesus spoke revealed the fact that He possesses a unique authority. In this respect His use of the word ἀμην ("verily") (from Hebrew אָמֵן = be firm) is significant. In all Jewish and Christian literature outside the Gospels wherever ἀμην or its equivalents are used, this occurs at the end of a sentence. But Jesus solemnly placed the ἀμην at the beginning of His declarations.

[1] T. Rees, "Authority", *International Standard Bible Encyclopaedia*, 1943 edn. ed. by James Orr. Cf. the words of Edwyn Earle Tilden (Jr.), "The Function of the Old Testament in the Sayings of Jesus—as recorded in the Synoptic Gospels", Th.D. thesis, Princeton, 1945, p. 278: "The authority of the prefigured Messiah is now (in Jesus) revealed and stands over and over against the authority of the Old Testament as the actualization of a purpose stands to its provisional expression."

And T. W. Manson correctly states: "The frequent and emphatic ἀμὴν λέγω ὑμῖν, 'Verily I say unto you', is enough to set Jesus as a teacher in a class apart from either prophets or scribes."[1]

The Old Testament prophets, when they spoke with authority, never dared to do so in their own name, but always made it explicitly known that they spoke with the authority of God. How often do we hear their words "Thus saith the Lord" resounding through the Old Testament! Only as messengers of the Almighty do they proclaim authoritative words. The scribes, again, in claiming authority for their declarations did so only by appealing to the Law or to the traditions of the elders, the תּוֹרָה שֶׁבַּל־פֶּה as they called it. At most their declarations were but deductions or applications of the written or oral Law.

Direct, final authority claimed

But Jesus, in absolute contrast to both the prophets and the scribes, speaks with direct, final authority. He never begins His declarations with "Thus saith the Lord" and neither appealed to any tradition nor sheltered Himself behind a respectable name.[2] In proclaiming as it were the new, perfect law of the kingdom in the Sermon on the Mount Jesus never says "God commands you" or "It is the law of God", but consistently and repeatedly declares: "Verily I say unto you."

He claims such absolute authority for His commandments that He concludes the Sermon on the Mount with the remarkable words: "Everyone therefore which heareth these words of mine, and doeth them, shall be likened unto a wise man, which built his house upon the rock: and the rain descended, and the floods came, and the winds blew, and beat upon that house; and it fell not: for it was

---

[1] *The Teaching of Jesus*, Cambridge, 1943, p. 106.

[2] The authority of Jesus does not depend upon any external credentials, but is involved in what He is. "The ambassador of an earthly king has credentials external to his person and his message, but not the ambassador in whom God Himself visits His people. His actions, like His words, speak for themselves" (James Denney, "Authority", *Dictionary of Christ and the Gospels*, ed. by James Hastings).

founded upon the rock. And every one that heareth these words of mine, and doeth them not, shall be likened unto a foolish man, which built his house upon the sand: and the rain descended, and the floods came, and the winds blew, and smote upon that house; and it fell: and great was the fall thereof" (Matt. vii. 24–7).

Familiar as these words are, they powerfully reflect our Lord's consciousness of supreme authority. And in Luke xxi. 33 this appears, if possible, even more clearly. For, whereas in the Old Testament it is said of the words of God that they, in contrast to all earthly things, endure for ever (Isa. xl. 6 f.), Jesus here declares: "Heaven and earth shall pass away: but my words shall not pass away." Only because He is indeed the Son of God, one with the Father (John x. 30), possessing with the Father absolute divine authority, could and did He speak thus.

Jesus acted with authority in a unique manner

But the Gospels show us further that our Lord did not reveal His authority just through speaking with authority. He consistently acted with authority in a supremely unique way.

He revealed His divine ἐξουσία over nature: "Jesus rebuked the wind and the raging of the water: and they ceased, and there was a calm" (Luke viii. 24).

He exercised authority over diseases and infirmities. To the woman who had been bound by infirmity for eighteen years He said: "Woman, thou art loosed from thine infirmity. And he laid his hands upon her: and immediately she was made straight, and glorified God."

He revealed his authority over the demoniac hosts, the powers of Satan: "And in the synagogue there was a man, which had a spirit of an unclean demon; and he cried out with a loud voice, Ah! what have we to do with thee, thou Jesus of Nazareth? art thou come to destroy us? I know thee who thou art, the Holy One of God. And Jesus rebuked him, saying, Hold thy peace, and come out of him. And when the devil had thrown him [the man] down in the midst, he came out of him, having done him no hurt. And amazement came upon all, and they spake together, one with another, saying, What is this word that with authority [ἐξουσία] and power he commandeth the unclean spirits, and they come out?" (Luke iv. 33-6).

Jesus also acted with authority towards men. When He announced Himself as the Fulfiller of Scripture in the synagogue in Nazareth, the Jews were all filled with wrath and determined to kill Him. They "rose up, and cast him forth out of the city, and led him unto the brow of the hill whereon their city was built, that they might throw him down headlong". Humanly speaking, there was no chance of escape. But Jesus, revealing his authority over men, "passing through the midst of them went his way" (Luke iv. 30).

In many other ways He revealed his authority over men. He claimed men, moral personalities, for Himself and His work, and demanded of them unconditional renunciation of all they possessed —yes, even of their very lives—that they might be His disciples. "Nothing is more unlike Jesus than to do violence to anyone's liberty, or to invade the sacredness of conscience and of personal responsibility; but the broad fact is unquestionable that, without breaking their wills, He imposed His own will upon them, and became for them a supreme moral authority to which they submitted absolutely and by which they were inspired."[1]

He went still further and demanded unconditional faith not only in His teachings or in His leadership but in Himself, and often declared that the eternal fate of man will depend on whether man exercised this unconditional faith in Him or not (Matt. x. 32, xi. 6).

He even forgave sins

He not only declared that He is the Way and the Life and that only through Him man can come to the Father, but already during His ministry He acted as the giver of salvation and Himself forgave sins. He did this so entirely in His own name that when doing it

[1] James Denney, "Authority", *Dictionary of Christ and the Gospels*, ed. by James Hastings.

He did not even mention the name of God. "Jesus did indeed claim (and exercise) rights which belong to God alone and which Judaism had never dared to attribute even to the Messiah, for in the Messianic Age forgiveness was to remain the prerogative of God (Isa. xliii. 25; Jer. xxxi. 34; Ezek. xxxvi. 25)."[1] And when the Pharisees exclaimed "This man blasphemeth" (Matt. ix. 3) and asked "Who can forgive sins but God alone?" our Lord, by forthwith healing the palsied man, provided the proof that He has the authority to do this which only God can do (cf. Mark ii. 10).

To give mercy is a divine prerogative. Thus when we see Jesus on the cross proclaiming to the repentant thief that mercy is given to him, we perceive once more the kingly ἐξουσία of Him who is the Son of God and who alone was able to say: "What things soever the Father doeth, these also doeth the Son likewise" (John v. 19).

The reactions of His contemporaries

Because our Lord possessed, claimed and exercised such absolute authority as we have seen in the previous pages, the question arises: to what extent did His contemporaries perceive and acknowledge His authority?

When we read through the Gospels seeking a reply to this, we are, on the one hand, amazed to see how much evidence there is showing that men did realize the uniqueness of our Lord's ἐξουσία, and on the other hand we feel how completely natural and inevitable this was.

Already at the beginning of our Lord's ministry people were "astonished at his teaching: for he taught them as having authority, and not as the scribes" (Mark i. 22). And when the servants that were sent by the Jewish leaders to spy on Jesus returned they declared that never did any man speak as this man (John vii. 46). Matthew states at the end of the Sermon on the Mount: "And it came to pass, when Jesus ended these words, the multitudes were astonished at his teaching: for he taught them as one having authority, and not as their scribes" (Matt. vii. 28 f.). He spoke

[1] Otto Borcherdt, *The Original Jesus*, English trans., London, 1933, p. 370.

with such authority during those days in Jerusalem before His crucifixion that even His enemies had unwillingly to acknowledge his ἐξουσία so that ultimately no man even dared ask Him any question (Mark xii. 34), but "the people all hung upon him, listening" (Luke xix. 48). They could not help perceiving that He spoke in a uniquely authoritative manner.

And when He exercised His authority in works of healing, in exorcizing demons or in working other miracles, individuals as well as crowds were amazed. Luke ix. 43 describes how, after Jesus had freed and healed the boy with the unclean spirit, the people "were all astonished at the majesty of God". Likewise, after He had healed the blind and dumb man "the multitudes were amazed and said, Is this the son of David?" (Matt. xii. 23). And after He had raised the dead son of the widow "fear took hold on all: and they glorified God, saying, A great prophet is risen among us: and, God hath visited his people" (Luke vii. 16).

Even the demons [1] acknowledged His supreme ἐξουσία. As Luke iv. 41 declares: "And demons also came out from many, crying out, and saying, Thou art the Son of God." This fact is vividly pictured in Mark v. 6–8: "And when he [the demoniac] saw Jesus from afar, he ran and worshipped him; and crying out with a loud voice, he saith, What have I to do with thee, Jesus, thou Son of the Most High God? I adjure thee by God, torment me not."

The enemies of Jesus fearing Him

The authority Jesus inherently possessed and revealed was so manifest and challenging that even His most deadly enemies dared not attack Him openly, "for they feared him" (Mark xi. 18). All they could do was to plot how to have Him destroyed secretly, and through sly questions to try to ensnare Him or to bring Him in disrepute with the multitudes who were still so fascinated by the manifestation of His ἐξουσία.

When Jesus, filled with holy wrath, cleansed the temple by force and thus exercised once more a prerogative which in the Old

[1] See our note on demon-possession in our *Commentary on the Gospel of Luke*, London and Grand Rapids, 1950, p. 174.

Testament belongs only to God Himself, all that the enraged Jewish rulers ventured to do was to ask Him: "By what authority doest thou these things? or who gave thee this authority to do these things?" (Mark xi. 28). At an earlier stage in the ministry they are so offended by His authoritative words and acts that they accuse Him of blasphemy,[1] saying that they *intend* to stone Him, "because that thou, being a man, makest thyself God" (John x. 33). But during those last days in Jerusalem before His crucifixion they ultimately had to acknowledge His authority even to such an extent that in Mark xii. 34 it is related that "no man after that durst ask him any question".

Crying to Jesus for mercy

While those who did not want to accept His authority were offended or enraged[2] against Him, many of the ordinary people, however, unreservedly acknowledged and accepted Him as their Mighty Helper. Often do we hear words uttered before Him such as these: "Have mercy on me, O Lord, thou son of David" (Matt. xv. 22), or we read descriptions such as that in Matthew viii. 2: "And behold, there came a leper and worshipped him, saying, Lord, if thou wilt, thou canst make me clean", or Matthew xv. 25: "she came and worshipped him, saying, Lord, help me."

The authority of Jesus and His disciples

It was, however, especially in the circle of the disciples that the supreme ἐξουσία of Jesus was acknowledged more and more unreservedly. Already in their act of forsaking everything to follow Him, this fact is revealed. And so often in their relations with Him during His ministry do we see how they perceived His divine authority. When on the sea of Galilee Peter witnessed the wonder-

---

[1] σκανδαλίζεσθαι (be offended) points especially to the fact that men "stumble at His claims", "find something in Him which they cannot get over", and refuse to accept His authority (cf. Matt. xv. 12)..

[2] As J. Denney has stated: "Jesus' authority is inherent in Himself and His actions, and cannot with a good conscience be repudiated by anyone who sees what He is" ("Authority", *Dictionary of Christ and the Gospels*, ed. by James Hastings).

working power of the Lord, he "fell down at Jesus' knees, saying, Depart from me; for I am a sinful man, O Lord" (Luke v. 8). And when Jesus one night came walking upon the water and had entered the boat and the wind ceased, Matthew xiv. 33 declares that "they that were in the boat worshipped him, saying, Of a truth thou art the Son of God". This acknowledgement of the authority of Jesus reached a climax when, near Caesarea Philippi, Peter, in the name of all of the disciples, in reply to the question of our Lord, declared: "Thou art the Christ, the Son of the living God" (Matt. xvi. 16).

After the resurrection

Naturally, after the resurrection, which was the final proof and vindication of the authority of our Lord, the disciples came to a much more complete realization of who and what He is. Matthew xxviii. 17 states that "when they saw him [the risen Lord], they worshipped him", and later even doubting Thomas, in absolute surrender, uttered those wonderful words before Jesus: "My Lord and my God" (John xx. 28). After the Ascension "they worshipped him, and returned to Jerusalem with great joy" (Luke xxiv. 52), knowing that all $\dot{\epsilon}\xi ov\sigma\iota a$ in heaven and earth had been given to Him and that He is and will be with them even unto the end of the world (Matt. xxviii. 18–20).

Obedient to the commands of their Risen Saviour, they waited for the Gift of the Holy Ghost, and from the day of Pentecost the authority of Jesus became for them, in and through the Spirit of God, more than ever a living, abiding reality. And throughout the Acts we see not only how the teachings of our Lord have final authority for the disciples and believers, but how the risen and glorified Lord Himself, in living reality, remains in God their supreme Head and Lord. On the day of Pentecost Peter declared: "This Jesus did God raise up, whereof we all are witnesses. Being therefore by the right hand of God exalted [and thus clothed with supreme $\dot{\epsilon}\xi ov\sigma\iota a$], and having received of the Father the promise of the Holy Ghost, he hath poured forth this which ye see and hear" (Acts ii. 32 f.). And a little later: "Let all the house of Israel therefore know assuredly, that God hath made him both Lord and Christ, this Jesus whom ye crucified" (Acts ii. 36).

So when they went into the world they not only proclaimed the teaching of Jesus but preached unto men the living Christ, their Sovereign Lord and Saviour who is ever with them, directing their lives and building His Church.

Before he was stoned Stephen said in the hearing of all his persecutors: "Behold, I see the heavens opened, and the Son of man standing on the right hand of God [the place of honour and authority]" (Acts vii. 56). And with his last breath under the storm of stones he called to the Lord, saying: "Lord Jesus, receive my spirit."

Even Saul of Tarsus, the relentless persecutor of the believers, ultimately, on the way to Damascus, meets the exalted Lord and henceforth acknowledges and accepts His absolute authority in complete surrender.

And so the living Son of God from the very beginning of the Christian Church not only acts as her King and Lord but is acknowledged and obeyed as such by all the apostles and believers, as is reflected in the book of Acts.[1]

The words of Peter in Acts x. 36, where he says "Jesus Christ is Lord of all", give typical expression to the place of absolute authority that was given to our Saviour in the earliest Church.[2]

---

[1] This New Testament book shows us also how "by His permanent spiritual presence in the Church, He (the Lord) enters into, inhabits and governs its whole life and determines for it what is true and right at every stage of its development" (cf. Forrest, *The Authority of Christ*, 202-3, quoted by T. Rees in *The International Standard Bible Encyclopaedia*, art. "Authority").

[2] James Denney has rightly remarked about this statement of Peter: "Simply as it is, this assertion of the sovereignty of Jesus covers all that is characteristic in historical Christianity" (*Jesus and the Gospel*, New York, 1908, p. 15).

NOTE

For a detailed study of the progressive self-revelation of Jesus as the Saviour clothed with absolute divine authority compare our *Commentary on the Gospel of Luke* (Marshall, Morgan and Scott, London, 1950, pages 172-229, 273-9 and 639-46).

II

THE AUTHORITY OF THE LORD AS PROCLAIMED IN THE EPISTLES AND REVELATION

HAVING seen the supreme character of the authority of Jesus as revealed in the Gospels and Acts, and turning to the rest of the New Testament, we find that from beginning to end the same Sovereign Lord is proclaimed. There is no gulf between the presentation of our Lord in these writings and of that found in the Gospel history. On the contrary, the consistent proclamation of every New Testament writing of Jesus as the Lord of all authority binds the whole New Testament together to form a remarkable unity.

The term "the Lord"

Of greatest importance here is the fact that the term ὁ κυριος ("the Lord") is used to designate Jesus throughout[1] the New Testament, and especially in the Epistles.

Among scholars a tremendous battle has been raging around this title ὁ κυριος. This was especially intensified by the publication of Bousset's two books, *Kyrios Christos*, 1913, and *Jesus der Herr*, 1916. Bousset's main contention was that for the disciples and first Christians in Jerusalem Jesus was only a mysterious apocalyptic person and that it was Paul who deified and elevated Him to the position of Lord. As explanation of how Paul came to do this Bousset maintained that the apostle of Tarsus had imbued the spirit of the Hellenistic mystery religions through the Church at

---

[1] Harnack says of the whole period from the time of Paul to that of Nicaea: "So fest wie der Name ὁ κύριος hat kein anderer an Christus gehaftet" (No other name has clung so closely to Christ as that of ὁ κύριος) (*Lehrbuch der Dogmengeschichte*, 4th edn., Tübingen, 1909, i, p. 203).

32 SUPREME AUTHORITY

Antioch and accepted Jesus as a cult-god just as the mystery-devotees had their cult-gods. And so the title ὁ κυριος was, according to Bousset, ascribed to Him and primitive Christianity completely changed. Although radical scholars like Morton Enslin[1] still to a great degree hold to Bousset's thesis, it has been discarded by all impartial scholars. Of especial significance in this respect is Edward Meyer's chapter on "Das Christentum und der Hellenismus" in his *Ursprung und Anfänge des Christentums*.[2] He proves conclusively that no Hellenistic influence of any importance is to be found in Paul or in the rest of the New Testament. Meyer felt so strongly on the subject that on page 316 he states that his whole three-volume work is aimed at eradicating the popular misconception that Paul and Christianity are a product of "Hellenism". Bousset's whole theory has thus fallen to the ground.

Regarding the meaning of ὁ κυριος[3] after all the investigations and discussions of the first fifty years of this century, we can safely accept the following statement of Gresham Machen: "An important fact has been established more and more firmly by modern research—the fact that the Greek word 'Kyrios' in the first century of our era was, wherever the Greek language extended, distinctly a designation of divinity."[4] The common usage of the word indeed

[1] *Christian Beginnings*, Harper and Brothers, New York, 1938, pp. 192 f.
[2] Berlin, 1921-3, iii, pp. 315-38.
[3] The word itself comes from κῦρος meaning "supreme power, authority"! (Liddell and Scott), "Gewalt", "Machtfüll", "Veranlassung", "Daher das adjektiv κύριος: machthabend, bes Gesetzskraft habend, rechtmäszig gültig, berechtigt, befugt, bevollmächtigt . . . κύριος ist der, der über etwas oder jemand verfügen kann" ("Authority", "plenitude of power", "cause". Hence the adjective κῦρος having power, having the force of law, legally binding, empowered, competent, invested with full power . . . κύριος is one who can dispose of something or somebody) (Foerster, *Theol. Wörterbuch zum N.T.*, ed. by G. Kittel, Stuttgart, 1938, iii. p. 1043).
In the New Testament the word is sometimes used in its profane sense of "lord and owner" (mostly of one who owns slaves or bond-servants). When our Lord was addressed during his ministry with the vocative κυριε it was mostly only a title of respect—due to any person of high standing. But when the absolute title ὁ κύριος is ascribed to Him, the situation entirely changes, as we shall presently see.
[4] This was the case not only in the mystery religions but also in the emperor-cult—the title being used of the emperor to designate him as divine (cf. the important discussion in A. Deissmann, *Light from the Ancient East*, 1927 Eng. edn., trans. from 4th German edn., 1922, pp. 349-60).

SUPREME AUTHORITY 33

persisted; the word still expressed the relation which a master sustained towards his slaves. But the word had come to be a characteristically religious term, and it is in the religious sense, especially as fixed by the Septuagint, that it appears in the New Testament.[1]

Designated as God

The last sentence is especially important, for we must remember that in the Septuagint the same term ὁ κύριος[2] was used on numerous occasions as the rendering not only of "Adonai" but of "Jahveh", the holiest name of the covenant God of Israel. There can accordingly be no doubt that the New Testament authors, by calling Jesus ὁ κύριος[3] (the Lord), thereby designated Him as God, one with the Father and the Holy Spirit, and thus with them possessing absolute ἐξουσία over all and everything.

This comes out clearly also in the fact that the New Testament authors often apply to our Lord Old Testament texts in which the original is stated of "Jahveh" (cf. Rom. x. 11; Phil. ii. 10; 1 Cor. i. 31, x. 17; 2 Tim. iv. 14; and Eph. iv. 8). In a number of cases Jesus is given even the name θεός (the highest name for God)— e.g. John xx. 28, where Thomas called Jesus "My Lord and my God"; and in John i. 1 are the well-known words "the Word was God". Also in Hebrews i. 8, 9 our Lord is twice called "God".

Apart from the use of these titles ὁ κύρις and θεος to designate

[1] *The Origin of Paul's Religion*, Macmillan, 1936, p. 308.
[2] Cf. Quell's article on the use of ὁ κύριος in the LXX (*Theol. Wörterbuch zum N.T.*, ed. by G. Kittel, Stuttgart, 1938, iii, pp. 1056–80).
[3] Foerster declares that the New Testament usage of ὁ κύριος as the title for Jesus points to nothing less than that He was believed in as the One to whom all ἐξουσία in heaven and on earth is given. He then continues by declaring: "Drückte κύριος dies aus, dann konnten die LXX-stellen, die vom κύριος sprachen, auf Jesus bezogen werden: in ihm handelt Gott so wie es das A.T. vom Kùrios aussagt" (If κύριος expressed this, then the Septuagint passages that mentioned κύριος could be brought into relation with Jesus; in Him God acts as the Old Testament declares of the Kùrios) (*Theol. Wörterbuch zum N.T.*, ed. by G. Kittel, Stuttgart, 1938, iii, p. 1094).

The title points to the "personhafte, rechtmäszige, umfassende Obmacht Gottes" (personal, lawful, comprehensive might of God) (*ibid.*, p. 1087), and so, when applied to our Lord, powerfully describes His all-inclusive divine lordship.

c

Jesus, there are many other declarations in the Epistles and Revelation in which the supreme authority of Jesus is proclaimed. Paul says of Him in Colossians ii. 9 f.: "in him dwelleth all the fulness of the Godhead bodily . . . [he] who is the head of all principality and power." And 1 Peter iii. 22 contains the words: "Jesus Christ who is at the right hand of God, having gone into heaven; angels and authorities and powers being made subject unto him." Paul gives expression to the same truth in Ephesians i. 20 ff., where he declares that God made Jesus "sit at his right hand in heavenly places, far above all rule, and authority, and power, and dominion, and every name that is named, not only in this world, but also in that which is to come: and he put all things in subjection under his feet, and gave him to be head over all things to the church". In this impassioned description of the absolute and all-comprehensive authority of Jesus Paul has brought together that which was the living faith of the earliest Church, the very foundation of Christianity. And he reiterates the same facts in Philippians ii. 9–11: "God highly exalted him, and gave unto him a name which is above every name: that in the name of Jesus every knee should bow, of things in heaven and things on earth and things under the earth, and that every tongue should confess that Jesus Christ is Lord, to the glory of God the Father."

In 1 Corinthians ii. 8 and James ii. 1 He is called the "Lord of Glory", an expression so often used of God in the Old Testament. In passages like 2 Corinthians i. 2, Galatians i. 3, and Romans i. 7 the equality and unity of the Father and the Son is clearly set forth. And in the words of 2 Corinthians xiii. 14—"The grace of the Lord Jesus Christ, and the love of God, and the communion of the Holy Ghost, be with you all"—the name of our Lord "is linked on a plane of absolute equality with that of God the Father and of the Holy Spirit as the source of all spiritual blessing".[1]

His divine authority accepted unreservedly

From this fact—viz. that the apostles and the first believers acknowledged the absolute deity of our Lord—it inevitably followed

---
[1] Boettner, *The Person of Christ*, Eerdmans, 1943, p. 26.

.that they unreservedly accepted His divine ἐξουσία. So, for instance, we find that Paul calls himself "the slave of Jesus Christ" (Gal. i. 1; Rom. i. 1), thereby giving expression to the complete character of his surrender to the authority of our Lord. Jude iv. calls Jesus "our only Master and Lord".

The living Lord of lords

And the supremely important fact to remember is that to the New Testament writers Jesus was not merely the Lord who on earth exercised divine authority during His ministry and after His resurrection ascended to heaven, leaving behind authoritative teachings. For them He is throughout the living Lord who, although exalted to the right hand of God, nevertheless is always with them in power and authority. To them Jesus was not the Jesus of so many modern theologians, namely one who is presented as having been just *a* or the greatest teacher.[1] No. To the New Testament Church Christ was the "King of kings and the Lord of lords" (Rev. xix. 16). And from this it follows naturally and inevitably that His teachings also had for them final authority and that they looked upon all His works and actions as divinely significant. Although they worshipped Him as exalted Lord, they did not lose interest in the historical facts of His life, death and resurrection, nor in His teaching.

The fact that the Gospels originated in the Early Church shows clearly what fundamental *rôle* preaching concerning the historical details of the Lord's life played. This is also reflected in Acts and the Epistles.

See, for instance, Paul's words in Colossians iii. 16: "Let the word of Christ [His teaching] dwell in you richly." In

---

[1] It cannot be emphasized too much that the authority ascribed to the Lord in the New Testament epistles is utterly different from that ascribed to authoritative rabbis or prophets. After their death only some of their well-known and accepted words were looked upon as authoritative. In the case of Jesus, however, He Himself, in *all* He did and said and in what He was and is, is honoured and worshipped by the New Testament writers as the Living Lord who possessed absolute authority.

1 Thessalonians v. 15 Paul says: "this we say unto you by the word of the Lord." And in 2 John ix. it is explicitly stated: "Whosoever goeth onward and abideth not in the teaching of Christ, hath not God: he that abideth in the teaching, the same hath both the Father and the Son." So we see that Jesus' words have the same authority as He Himself as Divine Person has for them.[1]

Final character of His authority

The fact that this authority is of a final character is brought out clearly by Hebrews i. 1 ff.: "God, having of old time spoken unto the fathers in the prophets by divers portions and in divers manners, hath at the end of these days spoken unto us in the Son, whom he appointed heir of all things, through whom also he made the ages; who, being the effulgence of his glory, and the impress of his substance, and upholding all things by the word of his power, when he had made purification of sins, sat[2] down on the right hand of the Majesty on high."

Note especially the words "God hath at the end of these days spoken unto us ἐν υἱῷ [in the Son]". When God speaks He speaks with divine authority. And because He has spoken ἐν υἱῷ (the ἐν emphasizing not the content of that which is spoken but the person) Christ Himself is clothed with divine ἐξουσία. And that this authority is absolute follows from the whole context in which

---

[1] In a certain sense it is true that "Das Christentum ist von Anfang an Buchreligion gewesen" (Christianity has from the commencement been a book religion) (Jülicher-Fascher, *Einleitung in das N.T.*, 7th edn. Tübingen, 1931, p. 451) in that the Old Testament was of fundamental authority for the first Christians. But it is even more true that there was "neben—unbewuszt sogar hoch über—Gesetz und Propheten, eine Autorität, durch deren Anerkennung man sich eben von den 'ungläubigen' Verehrern des Gesetzes und der Propheten schied. Dieser neue 'Kanon' ist Jesus Christus" (next to—(but) unconsciously much higher than—the law and the prophets, an authority through the recognition of which one separated oneself from the "unbelieving" worshippers of the law and of the prophets. This new "canon" is Jesus Christ) (*ibid.*, p. 458).

[2] "Das Sitzen zur Rechter Gottes bedeutet Mitregentschaft, also gottgleiche Würde, wie schon das Sitzen in Gottes Gegenwart an sich" (Being seated on the right hand of God means co-regency, i.e. dignity equal to God, as already sitting in God's presence postulates) (Foerster, *op. cit.*, p. 1088).

these words occur. It could not be more clearly proclaimed that Christ is the final[1] word of God to man, and so possesses ultimate authority in all He said,[2] did and is.

This, then, is the consistent teaching of the New Testament. We shall now briefly consider how the authority of Jesus was believed in and accepted by the Early Church after the time of the apostles.

[1] In the whole of the New Testament the Old Testament Scriptures and the Lord are "für Glauben und Leben das Fundament" (for faith and life the foundation) (Jülicher-Fascher, *op. cit.*, p. 459).

[2] According to Resch in 1 Tim. v. 18 "ist ebenfalls ein alttestamentliches Wort und ein Herrenwort gleichzeitig als γραφή eingeleitet" (an Old Testament word and a word of the Lord is likewise introduced simultaneously with γραφή) *Agrapha Aussercanonische Schriftfragmente*, 2nd edn., Leipzig, 1906, p. 89. This is therefore another striking illustration of the absolute authority ascribed to the words of the Lord in the New Testament.

III

THE AUTHORITY OF THE LORD AS BELIEVED IN AND ACCEPTED BY THE EARLY CHURCH

BY A systematic examination of our sources we find that the same absolute authority of the Lord that is so clearly revealed to us in the New Testament is ascribed to Him in the writings of the Apostolic Fathers and other Early Church writers. We need quote only a few of the many relevant statements of the Fathers to make this sufficiently clear.

In the epistle to the Corinthians, par. 16, Clement of Rome (A.D. 96) calls Jesus "the sceptre of the majesty of God", and often uses expressions such as in par. 50: "Jesus Christ our Lord [$\varkappa\upsilon\varrho\iota\text{o}\varsigma$]¹, to whom be glory for ever and ever." In the first paragraph of his epistle to the Ephesians Ignatius (A.D. 110) speaks of "the will of the Father and of Jesus Christ our God". In several other places he also explicitly calls Jesus "our God"² (using the supreme title $\theta\varepsilon\text{o}\varsigma$). See also the words in his epistle to the Ephesians, par. 18: "our God, Jesus the Christ". The same absolute acknowledgement of the divine authority of the Lord is reflected in the opening words of the ancient homily known as II Clement which begins as follows:

---

[1] Harnack declared concerning the belief of the Early Church: "So gewiss die Erlösung auf Gott selbst zurückgeführt wurde, so fest stand es,'dass sie durch Jesus (ὁ σωτὴρ ἡμων) vermittelt sei. Daher war der Glaube an Jesus auch für die Heiden-christen das Christenthum in verkürzter Gestalt. Jesus wird am häufigsten mit demselben Namen ὁ κύριος (ἡμων) bezeichnet ... wie Gott" (So surely as salvation was traced back to God Himself, so firmly was it established that it was mediated through Jesus (ὁ σωτὴρ ἡμων). Hence the belief in Jesus was for the heathen proselytes also Christianity in an abridged form. Jesus is most often designated by the same name, ὁ κύριος (ἡμων) ... as God.)

[2] Cf. the words of Pliny the Younger in his letter to Trajan in A.D. 112, saying of the Christians that they sing to Christ as to a God (*carmen dicere Christo quasi deo*) (*Epist.* x. 96).

"Brethren, we ought so to think of Jesus Christ as of God."[1] Polycarp, in his letter to the Church at Philippi (± A.D. 110), par. 2, declares: "Ye believed on Him that raised our Lord Jesus Christ from the dead and gave unto Him glory and a throne on His right hand; unto whom all things were made subject that are in heaven and that are on earth; to whom every creature that hath breath doeth service; who cometh as judge of quick and dead; whose blood God will require of them that are disobedient unto Him." And this same Polycarp about forty years later, when he stood before the magistrate in the arena of Smyrna and was demanded to "swear by the genius of Caesar and revile the Christ", replied unhesitatingly: "Fourscore and six years have I been His servant, and He hath done me no wrong. How then can I blaspheme my King who saved me?" (cf. *Martyrdom of Polycarp*, par. 9). In par. 21 of this letter there is that remarkable statement: "He [Polycarp] was apprehended . . . in the proconsulship of Statius Quadratus, but in the reign of the Eternal King Jesus Christ."

So we see now from various angles and in different modes of expression the supreme ἐξουσία of Jesus is repeatedly emphasized in a clear and dynamic way. Already from the fact that they worshipped and served Him as God, one with the Father, it followed that they unreservedly believed in and accepted His authority. For the idea of supreme authority is correlative to the notion of deity. In God is the highest, the ultimate ἐξουσία. Thus, where Jesus is worshipped, honoured and followed as truly God, it follows immediately that final authority is ascribed to Him in all He did, was and is.

Historical facts and teachings

We are therefore not at all surprised that also the *historical facts* concerning Jesus and *His teachings*[2] have final authority for all the apostolic and other Church leaders of those first centuries.

[1] This homily (called II Clement) is the oldest Christian sermon outside the New Testament that has come down to us in written form (cf. Harnack, *Lehrbuch der Dogmengeschichte*, i, p. 206).
[2] "The words of the Lord in the Early Church undoubtedly possessed unconditional authority" (Lietzmann, *The Founding of the Church Universal*, New York, 1938, p. 71).

Clement, in his epistle to the Corinthians, par. 13, for instance, says: "let us do that which is written", and then quotes a passage from the Old Testament and immediately after that declares: "remembering most of all the words of the Lord Jesus which He spoke, teaching forbearance and longsuffering: for thus He spoke: Have mercy, that ye may receive mercy . . . etc. [quoting words found in Matthew v. 7, vi. 14, vii. 1, 2, 9; Luke vi. 31, 36–8]." After quoting the words of Jesus he goes on to say: "With this commandment and these precepts let us confirm ourselves, that we may walk in obedience to His hallowed words, with lowliness of mind." And a few lines further on he writes: "Therefore it is right and proper, brethren, that we should be obedient unto God" (par. 14). From all this three facts emerge: (1) The Old Testament has absolute authority for Clement; (2) the words of Jesus also have alongside of the Old Testament final authority; (3) in the Old Testament as well as in the words of Jesus Clement sees the authority of God Himself.

These are no isolated statements of Clement. Again and again in his writings, as well as in those of the other Fathers, there occur expressions like "remember the words of Jesus our Lord" (Clement to the Corinthians, par. 46), "Let him that hath love in Christ fulfil the commandments of Christ" (par. 49), and God did "through Jesus Christ instruct us" (par. 59). Ignatius (Eph., par. 9) speaks of the Ephesian believers "being arrayed from head to foot in the commandments of Jesus Christ". In his letter to the Magnesians (par. 9) he uses the expression "Jesus Christ our only teacher". And Polycarp, writing to the Philippians, says: "walk in Jesus' commandments . . . remembering the words which the Lord spoke, as He taught: Judge not, that ye be not judged. Forgive, and it shall be forgiven to you. . . ." Barnabas (par. 2), again, speaks of "the new law of our Lord Jesus Christ". And *The Shepherd of Hermas* (par. 3) has the following remarkable words: "this great tree which overshadows plains and mountains and all the earth is the law of God which was given to the whole world; *and this law* is the Son of God preached unto the ends of the earth."

Here, in pictorial language, is described what was the living faith of the Christian Church during the first two centuries, namely: Christ, in unity with the Father, is, in all that He spoke, did, was and still is, the absolute authority.

New Testament writings accepted as authoritative

From this it followed spontaneously and inevitably that, in course of time and when the original witnesses of Jesus were no longer there, those writings[1] which were believed to contain the genuine teachings and history of and the authoritative proclamations concerning the Lord were accepted more and more consciously as clothed with final authority.[2]

Justin Martyr already spoke of "they who have recorded all that concerns our Saviour Jesus Christ" (*Ap.* i, 33, 67), and speaking of the written Gospel he declares: "I shall prove to you as you stand here that we have not believed empty fables, or words without foundation, but words filled with the Spirit of God, and great with power, and flourishing with grace." He could surely not have emphasized the divine authority of the writings concerning the Lord more clearly. In his *Dialogue with Trypho,* xlix, line 100, he even quotes Gospel words with the formula "it is written". (It is significant that a few lines earlier, while quoting the Gospel words preceding those he quoted with "it is written", he introduced them with "our Christ said".)

[1] It followed naturally that "seit der Herr und sein Evangelium dem Gläubigen nicht mehr unmittelbar erreichbar waren, muszten die beglaubigten Schriften über ihn und sein Werk an die leer gewordene Stelle rücken" (since the Lord and His Gospel were no longer immediately accessible to believers, the accredited writings about Him and His work had to advance to the place that had become empty) (Jülicher-Fascher, *op. cit.,* p. 458). "Die Evangelienbücher werden als Ersatz für mündliche Berichte geschätzt, so wie eine Gemeinde den Brief ihres Apostles als Ersatz für seinen, zeitweilig nicht zu erreichenden, persönlichen Zuspruch schätzte" (The books of the Gospels were valued as substitute for oral statements, just as a congregation valued the letter of their apostle as a substitute for his personal exhortation which was temporarily not to be obtained) (*ibid.,* p. 460).

[2] Jülicher-Fascher (*ibid.,* p. 461) dates II Clement about A.D. 145 and declares that in this writing already the New Testament writings (in which the Gospel of the Lord is incorporated) are placed on the same level of authority as the Old Testament.

Eusebius, *Historia Ecclesiastica*, iv, 23, incorporated a letter written by Dionysius of Corinth to Soter, Bishop of Rome, at about A.D. 170, in which Dionysius speaks of the Gospel writings as "the Lord's writing". A little later Irenaeus gives still clearer expression to the fact that the authoritative proclamation concerning the Lord of all authority is to be found in our four Gospels. He declares: "It is not possible that the Gospels can be either more or fewer in number than they are. For, since there are four zones of the world in which we live, and four principal winds, while the Church is scattered throughout all the world, and the pillar and ground of the Church is the gospel and the spirit of life; it is fitting that she should have four pillars ... the cherubim, too, were four-faced, and their faces were images of the dispensation of the Son of God. ... And therefore the Gospels are in accord with these things, among which Christ Jesus is seated ..." (*Adv. Haer.* iii, 11, 8). In iii, 16, 2, where he describes how the Lord is clearly and carefully proclaimed to us in the Gospels, he declares explicitly that the Holy Ghost spoke through the evangelists—thus claiming absolute authority for the writings in which the life, teachings and redeeming work of our Lord is described.

The living Lord Himself

At the time of Irenaeus it was thus axiomatically held that "Bücher sind es, die diesen unangreifbaren Kanon (ὁ κυριος) in unangreifbarer Form enthalten"[1] (It is in books that this unassailable canon (ὁ κυριος) is contained in an unassailable form). But for the Early Church the ultimate authority remained, above all, in the Lord Himself,[2] about whom these apostolic books proclaim the glad tidings of salvation. He was to the early Fathers the living Lord to whom unreserved obedience and love are due.

[1] *Op. cit.*, p. 474.
[2] Cf. the words in II Clement, par. 8: "The Lord saith in the Gospel" (followed by words quoted from Matthew and Luke). In several other places II Clement, before quoting New Testament passages, has the words: "The Lord saith." Cf. also Justin, *Ap.* i, chap. 12.

SPECIAL NOTE

THE SIGNIFICANCE OF THE FACT OF THE AUTHORITY OF JESUS

THE FACT *as such* that Jesus possesses supreme divine authority is, even apart from its being acknowledged by all New Testament authors and by the whole of the Early Church, of the greatest significance for the study of the making of the New Testament. For it gives us the assurance that the Lord of all authority would have seen to it that, through the working of His power, an adequate and completely reliable account of and an authentic proclamation concerning the significance of His life and work were written and preserved for the ages to come. Because the revelation of God in Christ was complete and ἐφάπαξ, "einmalig" (once and for all), it follows logically that the Lord to whom all authority in heaven and on earth is given would have regulated the history of the Early Church in such a way that the canon of the New Testament would be genuine and all-sufficient. In the section on the authority of the apostles we hope to show through what main medium our Saviour brought this about.

(B) The Authority of the Apostles in the New Testament and the Early Church

We have seen how the New Testament reveals and proclaims the supreme authority of the Lord and how the Early Church believed in and accepted His authority as final. When we now investigate what authority, if any, was ascribed to His apostles, we find:—

    I. The Lord Himself called, equipped and sent forth the apostles.

   II. The apostles themselves claimed to possess and exercised authority.

  III. The authority of the apostles was acknowledged in the Early Church.

I

THE LORD HIMSELF CALLED, EQUIPPED AND SENT FORTH THE APOSTLES

THE GOSPELS show us that, soon after Jesus' baptism and the temptation in the wilderness, He began, at the commencement of His public ministry, to call certain men to follow Him (Matt. iv. 18 f.). Probably within a few months a group of disciples had already gathered round Him, seeing in Him at least a unique teacher, and following Him while He was teaching the multitudes and performing His works of healing. At first all those that followed Jesus were called merely His "disciples", but "it came to pass in these days, that he went into the mountain to pray; and he continued all night in prayer to God. And when it was day, he called his disciples: and he chose from them twelve, whom also he named apostles"[1] (Luke vi. 12 f.).

By a deliberate[2] action, according to the Gospels, our Lord created

---

[1] Our sources give us the fullest right to agree with Rengstorf that it is certain that "nicht nur der Apostolat in der Sache auf Jesus zurück geht, sondern dasz auch der Apostelname von ihm gebraucht worden ist" (not only is the apostolate as such traced back to Jesus but that also the name apostle was used by Him) (*Theol. Wörterbuch zum N.T.*, edited by Kittel, i, p. 429, art. "ἀπόστολος").

[2] Even Harnack says of the attempts made to disprove the historicity of the fact that Jesus appointed the chosen Twelve to be His disciples: "criticism is here running on false lines" (*Origin of the New Testament*, London, 1925, p. 45). He goes on to say: "There also appears to be no special reason to doubt that Jesus during His lifetime sent out twelve disciples on a mission in Palestine and that they actually undertook this mission and returned to Him again. All in all, sayings of Jesus must have existed that referred to the disciples as sent out on the mission, and that offered them the prospect of the highest authority, and of even Messianic powers when the 'Kingdom' was established. On this supposition alone can we explain the authority of the Twelve in the Church" (p. 45). But then he makes the groundless statement (cf. our discussion, *infra*): "For the Twelve after our Lord had departed from them and was glorified, played in reality an insignificant *rôle*.

SUPREME AUTHORITY 47

out of the wider circle of disciples a group of men who henceforth formed a definite unit and to whom alone He gave the name "apostles".

The derivation of the word "apostle"

Now the word ἀπόστολος is derived from the verb ἀποστέλλω, which has as its simplest meaning "to send forth" (cf. Rengstorf in Kittel's *Theologisches Wörterbuch zum N.T.*, i, art. "ἀποστέλλω"). The ἀπο serves, however, as a strengthening of the idea of "sending" and also as a sign that there is a purpose[1] attached to the "sending". The result is therefore that ἀποστέλλω easily lent itself to be used of sending somebody to represent the sender authoritatively. "Schon die Formel ἀπεσταλμένοι ὑπο τοῦ βασιλέως verbindet mit dem Gedanken der Sendung den weiteren der mit dieser verbundenen Autorisation des Gesendeten. Die damit gekennzeicheten Männer sind geradezu die Vertreter ihres Monarchen und seiner Autorität" (already the expression ἀπεσταλμένοι ὑπο τοῦ βασιλέως coupled with the idea of sending the authorization bound with this of them that are sent). The men thus designated are literally the substitute for their King and his authority (*ibid.*).

This use of ἀποστέλλω was, however, not confined to the secular-legal sphere, but reached its climax when it became the *terminus technicus* for the communication of religious-ethical power and authority. Especially among the Greek cynics ἀποστέλλειν was

---

This is only intelligible on the assumption that an express command of Jesus to begin a mission in grand style after His death did not exist. As a matter of fact, the Twelve remained in Jerusalem and, apart from awaiting the time when they would take up their office in the coming Kingdom, the building up of the Church in Jerusalem, of which task they were, moreover, soon relieved by James, the Lord's brother, remained the sole object of their existence" (pp. 45 f.). We shall see what a different picture Acts gives us of the activity of the Twelve and how the early Fathers ascribed vigorous activity to the apostles, and how all available evidence militates against this statement of Harnack.

[1] Moulton and Milligan quote an interesting sentence from an Oxyrhinichus papyrus in which ἀποστέλλω is used in the sense of "sent for a definite purpose", and they say of this usage that it "may illustrate the frequent New Testament sense of 'commissioning'—e.g. Matt. xi. 10, xiii. 41; John xx. 31; Rev. i. 1" (*Vocabulary of the Greek Testament, Illustrated from the Papyri and Other Non-literary Sources*, London, 1914–29, art. "ἀποστέλλω").

used of "der Bevollmächtigung durch die Gottheit" (the giving of supreme authority by the Divinity) (*ibid.*). But also authors like Epictetus, Irenaeus and Philo used it in this sense (*ibid.*), thus proving that it was a well-known usage in the Greek world in New Testament times. This does not, however, mean that ἀποστέλλω was used only in this religious-ethical sense. On the contrary, it continued to be used also with the original simpler meanings such as "send forth" or "send forth as a representative merely of an earthly ruler or of any other human person". Only out of the context in which it occurs can it be discovered with what connotation the word is used in a given instance.

In the Septuagint ἀποστέλλω is used about seven hundred times. Mostly to translate שָׁלַח. Here, too, it is used with different shades of meaning, from the simplest and secular to a sublime religious sense such as in Isaiah vi. 8. Here God asks: "Whom shall I send, and who will go for us?" And the context clearly shows that He sought someone whom He could send forth, clothed with authority to act as His messenger.

We must further note that ἀποστέλλω [1] differs in meaning from πέμπω. For while in πέμπω we have a general term pointing only to the sending as such, in ἀποστέλλω expression is given to the fact "dasz die Sendung unter einem ganz bestimmten, einmaligen und einzigartigen Gesichtspunkt erfolgt, einem Gesichtspunkt, der nicht nur Absender und Empfänger in Beziehung setzt, sondern gerade auch den, der gesandt wird, oder das, was Gegenstand der Sendung ist, aus der Situation heraus mit dem Sendenden verbindet" (that the mission takes place under a very definite, unique and peculiar aspect, an aspect that not only puts the sender and recipient in relation to each other, but actually also, arising from the situation, connects him who is sent, or that which is the object of the mission, with the sender) (*ibid.*). And from this we can clearly understand why it became freely used to point to the

---

[1] Abbot-Smith gives as meaning of ἀποστέλλω: (1) to send with a commission or on service; (2) to send away, dismiss (only a few times in this sense in the New Testament (*Manual Greek Lexicon of the New Testament*, 3rd edn., London, 1937). And πέμπω = "send".

fact that with the "sending" is connected a special "charge" or commission and a full authorization given by the one who sends.

ἀποστέλλω is used about one hundred and thirty times in the New Testament. And here, too, except in a few cases in the writings of John, we see the definite distinction between πέμπειν, where the stress lies merely on the sending as such, and ἀποστέλλειν, where the emphasis is placed on the fact that the sending is done with a definite purpose.

Rengstorf declares that in John ἀποστέλλω is used of Jesus "wo es sich um die Begründung seiner Autorität in Gottes Autorität als der Autorität des für seine Worte und Werke Verantwortlichen und sich für ihr Recht und ihre Wahrheit Verbürgenden handelt"[1] (where it treats of the foundation of His authority in God's authority, as the authority of one that is responsible for his words and works and that guarantees their right and their truth) (*op. cit.*, *p.* 404). Where, however, our Lord speaks in John of the Father as ὁ πεμψας με He points only, says Rengstorf, to the fact that God is the One who sent Him, *no special* stress being laid upon the idea of "sending with authority".

A few scholars contend that a close study of the Johannine writings shows that the author uses πέμπω and ἀποστέλλω with the same meaning of "to send with mandatory power, with authority to act as the representative of the sender" (cf. W. F. Howard, *Christianity According to St. John*, London, 1943, pp. 25 f.). The reason why he does not stress the distinction in meaning between the two verbs may, so it is conjectured, possibly be that John did not live in the LXX world of language so much as the other New Testament authors and knew Greek merely as one who had as

---

[1] Cremer-Kögel held the same views as Rengstorf holds here. Cf., for example, their words: "Dasz Jesus gesendet sei von Gott, will und soll den Auftrag, den er auszurichten hat, u.d. Autorität, die hinter ihm steht, anzeigen, John iii. 34: ὅν ἀπέστειλεν ὁ θεὸς τὰ ῥήματα τοῦ θεοῦ λαλεῖ (That Jesus was sent by God must and shall indicate the commission that He is to execute and the authority that stands behind Him) (*Biblisch-Theol. Wörterbuch der Neutestamentlichen Gräzität*, 10th edn., 1915, pp. 1018 ff.). He also differentiates between the meaning of πέμπω and ἀποστέλλω (*ibid.*).

mother-tongue Aramaic and who had to learn Greek only as a foreign language. He then, so it is suggested, rendered the Hebrew word שָׁלַח much more freely either by πέμπω or by ἀποστέλλω. Whether this is the case or not, there seems, nevertheless, no ground to suppose that John did not use ἀποστέλλω uniformly[1] to express the idea of sending with a purpose and with authority. The only difference between his usage and that in the other New Testament writers seems to be that he used πέμπω also (at least in a few cases)[2] with the meaning of "send as a שָׁלַח".[3] The Johannine writings do thus not weaken the force of ἀποστέλλω, but stress the fact of the "sending with authority and as representative of the sender" so much that even πέμπω, in a number of cases, seems to be used with a similar connotation.

It can therefore safely be said concerning the use of ἀποστέλλω that it bears practically the same meaning here as in the writings of the cynics, of Philo, and of other Greek orders in so far as it stresses the divine authorization of those sent out (here, in the service of the Kingdom of God).

But the *noun* ἀπόστολος presents more complications in its usage in the Greek-speaking world. For although, as we have seen, the *verb* ἀποστέλλω was widely used in the Hellenistic world to describe the idea that someone is sent by God (or by a deity) as His representative with power and authority to speak and act

---

[1] Even in xviii. 24 the verb is used with the sense of authoritative sending in so far as Annas sent Him officially for formal trial to Caiaphas (cf. Plummer, *The Gospel According to St. John, ad loc.*).

[2] A study of John's use of πέμπω and ἀποστέλλω shows clearly that whereas he always uses ἀποστέλλω in the sense of authoritative and purposive sending, he often uses πέμπω in the ordinary sense of "send". To us it seems that, after all, John did take into account the difference in meaning between the two verbs. Only in a number of cases did he extend to πέμπω the same meaning as ἀποστέλλω has.

[3] Cf. Howard, *op. cit.*, p. 25, where he writes, for instance: "The term 'He who sent me' is in this Gospel a divine title, and when the *Auctor ad Hebraeos* called Jesus 'the Apostle of our Confession' (Heb. iii) he expressed in one noun what St. John proclaims in a verbal phrase on almost every page. It sums up all the prerogatives and functions of prophecy in the unique mission of Him who came from the bosom of the Father."

SUPREME AUTHORITY 51

on His behalf, the noun[1] was used for "a fleet", "an expedition", "a messenger" (in the ordinary sense), or "one sent on a mission"—but seemingly never in the sense of "one sent by God with divine authority". Thus Rengstorf declares concerning the Greek-speaking world: "Die ältere Zeit kennt nichts, was man mit dem nt. lichen Apostel in Parallele setzen könnte" (Antiquity knows nothing that can be placed parallel to the New Testament apostle) (*op. cit.*, p. 408).

The Jewish Aramaic background

But when we turn to the Jewish-Aramaic background things are different. We find that soon after the exile the Jews began the practice of sending out certain of their members with definite charges which they had to fulfil as representatives of and clothed with the right and authority of the "holy community" who sent them. This became so especially when the scribes or rabbis began to play such an important *rôle* in the Jewish life. For the rabbis as a group, looking upon themselves as representatives of the community of the "holy people", often sent persons (mostly men from their own group) to other Jews (especially in the *diaspora*) with the commission to teach them certain truths[2]. The one they sent was given full power and authority to teach and act as the representative of the community of the holy nation of God, and the rabbis used

[1] Moulton and Milligan say of ἀπόστολος: "It is not easy to point to an adequate parallel for the New Testament usage of this important word, but it may be noted that in *Herod.* i, 21 (cf. v, 38) it is found—'messenger', 'envoy', and with the same meaning in LXX 3 *Regn.* xiv, 6" (*Vocabulary of the Greek Testament, Illustrated from the Papyri and Other Non-literary Sources*, London, 1914–29, art. "ἀπόστολος,"). They also show that, apart from its use in Attic inscriptions, as *Syll.* cliii (325 B.C.)—'fleet', 'naval expedition'—ἀπόστολος is used for a 'ship' in *P. Oxy.* cxi, 522, ii/AD (*ibid.*).
[2] Harnack says of the Jewish שְׁלוּחִים : "they were authoritative officials who collected contributions from the Diaspora for the temple and kept the Churches in touch with Jerusalem and with each other" (*Expansion of Christianity*, i, p. 409).

to say [1] שְׁלוּחוֹ שֶׁל אָדָם כְּמוֹתוֹ, which means "the one sent by a person is as this person himself".

But of course this was the case only within the limits of the commission given to the person who is sent. Men thus sent were called the שְׁלוּחִים.

Rengstorf rightly stresses the fact that "In ihrer Bezeichnung als שְׁלוּחִים erfolgt also weder die Beschreibung der Tatsache ihrer Aussendung noch eine Andeutung eines besonderen ihnen zuteil gewordenen Auftrags, sondern allein die Feststellung der Form der Sendung, d.h. die Feststellung ihrer Autorisation. Das ist das Entscheidende, während die Aufgabe als solche für die Qualität als שָׁלִיחַ in keiner Weise von Bedeutung ist[2]" (In their designation as שְׁלוּחִים there thus follows neither the description of the fact of their mission nor an indication of a special commission assigned to them, but merely the confirmation of the form of the mission, i.e. the confirmation of their authorization. This is the decisive element, while the commission as such is in no way of importance for the capacity or quality as שָׁלִיחַ).

Saul of Tarsus was sent to Damascus as a שָׁלִיחַ in this sense—clothed with full authority to act in the name of the Jerusalem Sanhedrin (Acts ix. 1).

It is, however, remarkable that although the Jews had these שְׁלוּחִים who were sent to other Jews, they did not have any *missionaries* who were clothed with the authority to teach or act in the name of the Jewish rabbis or community among non-Jewish people. There were indeed many Jewish individuals in New Testament times who did what we call "missionary work", but they acted in their own names as private individuals and were thus not missionaries "in the technical sense of people sent with the commission to teach those outside the holy community". Thus in the Jewish world, too, there is nothing[3] exactly parallel to

[1] Rengstorf, *op. cit.*, p. 415.
[2] *Op. cit.*, p. 414.
[3] As Rengstorf declares: "so gewisz das ältere Judentum bereits eine Fülle von verschiedenen Arten von שְׁלוּחִים gekannt hat so gewisz hat es diese Bezeich-

SUPREME AUTHORITY

the Christian "apostles", who, although they were שְׁלוּחִים, were pre-eminently sent to be *missionaries* and not just שְׁלוּחִים in the rabbinical sense.

The meaning of "apostle" in the New Testament

But notwithstanding the fact that neither in the Greek nor in the Hebrew world we have exact equivalents to the New Testament ἀπόστολος, the meaning given to the verb ἀποστέλλω in the Greek world and the similar type of meaning borne by the Hebrew noun שְׁלוּחִים[1] help us to see the meaning of the term ἀπόστολος[2] in the New Testament—namely, one chosen and sent with a

nung gerade nicht mit der missionarischen Tätigkeit seiner Glieder verbunden" (so surely as the older Judaism already knew an abundance of several kinds of שְׁלוּחִים, so surely it indeed never associated this designation with the missionary activities of its members) (*op. cit.*, p. 418). Regarding those Jews who did try to win non-Jews to the Jewish faith he says that "in Zusammenhang mit ihnen die Worte שָׁלַח und ἀποστέλλειν keinerlei Rolle spielen. Ihre Arbeit vollzog sich also ohne Autorisation durch die Gemeinde in engeren Sinne und trug ihr gegenüber durchaus private Character, ohne dasz sie dadurch an Umfang und Bedeutung verloren hatte" (in association with them the words שָׁלַח and ἀποστέλλειν play no part. So their work was accomplished without authorization by the congregation, it bore a private character throughout, without its having lost scope and importance because of this) (*id.*).

[1] J. B. Lightfoot already in 1865 wrote: "With the later Jews, and it would appear also with the Jews of the Christian era, the word was in common use. It was the title borne by those who were despatched from the mother-city by the rulers of the race on any foreign mission, especially such as were charged with collecting the tribute paid to the temple service. After the destruction of Jerusalem the 'apostles' formed a sort of council about the Jewish patriarch, assisting him in his deliberations at home, and executing his orders abroad. Thus in designating His immediate and most favoured disciples 'apostles' our Lord was not introducing a new term, but adopting one which from its current usage would suggest to His hearers the idea of a highly responsible mission" (*Epistles to the Galatians*, pp. 90 f.).

[2] The word appears seventy-nine times in the New Testament (twenty-nine times in Paul, twenty-eight times in Acts, six times in Luke, once in Matthew, once in Mark, once in John, once in Hebrews, once in 1 Peter, twice in 2 Peter, once in Jude, three times in Revelations) and has uniformly the meaning of "one sent as authorized representative". In most cases it is used of the Twelve and Paul as the especial שְׁלוּחִים of the Lord. In a few cases, however, it is used with a wider meaning—e.g. to point to the fact that certain persons are the authorized missionaries or delegates of a community (*vide infra*).

special commission as the fully authorized representative of the sender. Especially in John xiii. 16 (the only place in which John uses the word) it appears clearly how ἀπόστολος must be understood in the sense of one who is "mit der Vertretung von Person und Sache eines andern rechtsgültig beauftragt" (validly commissioned with the representation of the person and case of another party) (*op. cit.*, p. 422). It is thus in meaning sharply contrasted to ἄγγελος, which designates merely a messenger, and also to κηρυξ, which means only a herald.[1]

The Lord preparing His disciples for their mission

By calling the twelve men whom He chose out of the wider circle of disciples by the name "apostles" (שְׁלוּחִים) and not merely "messengers" or "heralds", Jesus thus made it clear that they were to be His delegates whom He would send with the commission to teach and to act in His name and on His authority. That this was indeed what He meant is shown by the whole history of His dealings with the Twelve.[2]

In all the four Gospels we see that our Lord at a comparatively early date during His public ministry began to teach His disciples that the time would come when He would no longer be with them and that they would have to go into the world as His witnesses and representatives. Therefore He made them first His special intimate disciples (μαθηται > μανθανω = to teach) to teach them

---

[1] The term "apostle" (ἀπόστολος) is more definite than "messenger" (ἄγγελος), in that the apostle has a special mission and is the commissioner of the person who sends him. This distinction holds good both in classical and Biblical Greek (Alfred Plummer, "apostle", Hastings' *Dictionary of the Apostolic Church*, Edinburgh, 1916, i. p. 82). J. B. Lightfoot also declares: "Applied to a person, ἀπόστολος denotes more than ἄγγελος. The 'apostle' is not only the messenger but the delegate of the person who sends him. He is entrusted with a mission, has powers conferred upon him" (*Epistle to the Galatians*, Macmillan, 1865, p. 89). Cf. Justin, I *Apol.* xii, where he says Jesus is both "Son and Apostle of God the Father".

[2] Cremer-Kögel writes that giving the name "apostles" to the Twelve designated them as the Lord's "Reichsboten und grundlegenden Zeugen" (member of parliament and foundationlaying witnesses) (*Biblisch-Theologisches Wörterbuch der Neutestamentlichen Gräzität*, 10th edn., 1915, p. 1019).

SUPREME AUTHORITY 55

intensively and lead them into the secrets of His kingdom so that at the appointed time they would be able to act as His שְׁלוּחִים[1]. By what He did and said and by the experiences He made them undergo He was continually busy to prepare them for the task of acting as His apostles. Most essential of all was that they should learn to know Him as the heavenly Messiah and the Son of God. And it is significant that after the episode near Caesarea-Philippi, when the disciples explicitly expressed their belief that He is the Christ, the Son of the living God, our Lord immediately announced that before long He would have to suffer and be killed (Matt. xvi. 21 ff.). More than ever before, He now, during the second period of His ministry, concentrated on teaching His disciples.

The disciples having practical experience of acting as apostles

But apart from His instruction of the disciples and His revealing Himself ever more fully to them the Gospels show us how our Lord adopted still another method to prepare them to become His שְׁלוּחִים. He gave them the opportunity of actually practising to be His legitimate representatives. As Luke describes it in ix. 1–10: "And he called the twelve together, and gave them power and authority (ἐξουσία) over all demons, and to cure diseases. And he sent[2] them forth (ἀπέστειλεν) to preach the kingdom of God,

[1] "Christ chose them in the first instance (Mark iii. 14) 'that they might be with him', to be educated and trained, 'and that he might send them forth to preach' and do works of mercy. Instruction is the main thing, and 'disciples' is the usual designation (in the Gospels); mission work (during our Lord's ministry) is secondary and temporary. After the Ascension their mission work (however) becomes primary and permanent. Apostleship is now the main thing; in Acts 'apostles' is the dominant appellation, and in the Epistles 'disciples' are not mentioned. Instead of being led and guided, the Twelve have now become leaders and guides; or rather, instead of having a visible guide, they now have an invisible one, instead of Jesus, 'the Spirit of Jesus' (Acts xvi. 7), who helps them to lead others" (A. Plummer, *op. cit.*, pp. 82 f.).

[2] To point once more to the significance of the verb ἀποστέλλω, we quote Cremer-Kögel: "ἀποστέλλω absenden, entsenden, nämlich zu einem bestimmten Zweck, wodurch es sich von πέμπειν unterscheidet, das nur die Übermittlung bezeichnet" (ἀποστέλλω to send off, to despatch, namely for a definite purpose, and thereby it differs from πέμπειν which merely denotes transmission) (*op. cit.*, p. 1018).

and to[1] heal the sick. ... And [said Jesus to them] as many as receive you not, when ye depart from that city, shake off the dust from your feet for a testimony against them. And they departed, and went throughout the villages, preaching the gospel, and healing everywhere.... And the apostles [ἀπόστολοι], when they were returned, declared unto him what things they had done. And he took them, and withdrew apart to a city called Bethsaida." From this we clearly see how our Lord deliberately sent them out as His שְׁלוּחִים.

It is significant that Luke in ix. 10 calls them "apostles", but in verse 14, where they have once more assumed the rôle of followers and learners, he again calls them "disciples" (μαθηταί). This is still more noticeable in Matthew x. 1 ff. Verse 1 (a) reads "and he called unto him his twelve disciples [μαθηταί]". In the rest of the verse is described how Jesus gave them authority, and after that, in verse 2, the Twelve are called "apostles". But in xii. 1, where they are once more merely followers of the Lord, they are again called "disciples". This shows clearly that the Gospel writers were fully aware of the significant meaning of the word ἀπόστολος. Mark, just as Matthew, calls the Twelve by the name "apostles" only once, and that also in his description of the episode of the sending of the "twelve" by Jesus.

Harnack on a wrong track

Harnack has therefore given a wrong interpretation of facts by declaring that Matthew, Mark and John are all "ignorant of 'apostle' as a designation of the Twelve" and that "the primitive Church rested their dignity, not on their position as apostles, but as the twelve disciples (chosen by Jesus)". (*The Expansion of Christianity in the First Three Centuries*, London, 1904, vol. i, p. 399).

[1] It is important to note that the Lord gave His apostles the power and the authority not merely to teach and preach but also to act as His representatives in such a way that the power of the divine rule could through them also become effective.

Cf. also his words: "the term (ἀπόστολος) cannot be sharply restricted at all; for as God appoints prophets and teachers in the Church so also does He appoint apostles to be the front rank therein, and since such charismatic callings depend upon the Church's needs, which are known to God alone, their numbers are not fixed" (p. 401). In a certain sense this is true, but not in the way Harnack pictures it in his different works where he discusses this subject. Take, for instance, his statement that the fact that afterwards the Twelve ranked "in history as the twelve apostles, and indeed as *the* apostles, was a result brought about by Paul; and paradoxically enough this was brought about by him in his efforts to fix the value of his own apostleship" (p. 403). Harnack, however, could not point to one real fact to prove this theory. And, as we have already seen and shall presently see, all the evidence we find in the New Testament and in the Early Church shows overwhelmingly that Harnack has given an utterly distorted view of the facts regarding the authority of the primitive apostles. His theories concerning this matter are extremely subjective.

Jesus sent them as apostles

In Matthew's longer description of the sending of the Twelve the following words in our Lord's instructions are of exceptional importance as showing how He sent them as His "apostles" (שְׁלוּחִים) in the fullest sense of the term: "These twelve Jesus sent forth [ἀπέστειλεν], and charged them, saying [note the words 'sent forth' and 'charged'] . . . preach. . . . Heal the sick, raise the dead, cleanse the lepers, cast out demons [all these are things that Jesus Himself had been doing]. . . . if the house be worthy, let your peace come upon it: but if it be not worthy, let your peace return to you. And whosoever shall not receive you, nor hear your words, as ye go forth out of that house or that city, shake off the dust off your feet. Verily I say unto you, It shall be more tolerable for the land of Sodom and Gommorrah in the day of judgement, than for that city [this means their words have the same authority than His own divine words]. . . . But when they deliver you up, be not anxious how or what ye shall speak: for it shall be given you in that hour what ye shall speak [here our Lord's words are going beyond the sphere of the mission on which He was sending them at that time and points to the time when He will no longer be with them]" (Matt. x. 5 ff.).

In verse 40 our Lord explicitly declares that they are appointed to be His שְׁלוּחִים, by saying: "He that receiveth you receiveth me."

In Mark vi we also see how explicitly the significance of the term "apostles" is brought out. In vi. 1 "his *disciples* follow him" (here they are the learners, following the Teacher). But in vi. 30, after Jesus had given them authority and had sent them forth and they had gone on their mission, we read: "And the *apostles* gather themselves together unto Jesus; and they told him all things, whatsoever they had done, and whatsoever they had taught." (Here they are the שְׁלוּחִים who, after they have taught and acted as the Sender's representatives, give account of the way in which they fulfilled the charge He had given them.)

The apostles were still learners

The fact that Matthew and Mark call the Twelve "apostles" only in connection with their being sent out by the Lord to act in His name and with His power and authority does not mean that they were only temporarily His apostles. For as is shown by Luke (vi. 12 f.), when our Lord chose them from the wider circle of disciples He appointed them to be His apostles permanently. They are also, apart from the cases in the description how they were sent out, called apostles several times during the later part of the Gospel history (cf. Luke xvii. 5, xxii. 14, xxiv. 10). The reason why they are nevertheless mostly called "disciples" before the resurrection seems to be that, apart from the special occasions when Jesus sent them out to act as His שְׁלוּחִים, they were, although His apostles, still most of the time with Him as "learners".

As the end of our Lord's ministry on earth approached He more

SUPREME AUTHORITY 59

and more explicitly taught His disciples that they who were already appointed by Him as His apostles would have to *act* as His apostles. Think, for instance, of those tremendous words of His to the Twelve in Matthew xviii. 18: "Verily I say unto you, What things soever ye shall bind on earth shall be bound in heaven: and what things soever ye shall loose on earth shall be loosed in heaven." Could Jesus more clearly have expressed the fact that to the apostles is given the power and authority to act as His representatives, His שְׁלוּחִים? These words remind us of the similar statement our Lord had made after Peter's confession near Caesarea-Philippi when He said to Peter as the leader and chief representative of the apostles: "thou art Peter, and upon this rock I will build my church; and the gates of Hades shall not prevail against it. I will give unto thee the keys of the kingdom of heaven; and whatsoever thou shalt bind on earth shall be bound in heaven: and whatsoever thou shalt loose on earth shall be loosed in heaven" (Matt. 16: 18).

T. W. Manson holds to the opinion that our Lord, in calling and sending the Twelve, had in view only "the creation of a circle of intimate companions, and the establishment of a missionary body",[1] and that He did not mean to give them a place of special dignity and authority in the Church. But what we have already seen regarding the significance of the term ἀπόστολος and all other available evidence in the New Testament and in the Early Church (*vide supra et infra*) radically contradicts his views. Our Lord did most certainly intend His apostles to be His missionaries, but in such a way that they should be the authoritative foundation layers of His Church. The fact that the Early Church acknowledged the supreme authority of the apostles (Paul included) was not, as Manson thinks,[2] a "calamity and the complete reversal of the original intention of Jesus", but was in complete accord with our Lord's action regarding the apostles, and was, next to the acknowledgement of the authority of the Lord Himself, the most powerful factor in the making of the New Testament and in saving the Church from complete disintegration under the influence of

[1] *The Teaching of Jesus*, Cambridge, 1943, p. 241.
[2] *Ibid.*, p. 242.

the gnostic and other philosophies and religions of the first two centuries. Undoubtedly the Church did, especially from the end of the second century onwards, in some respects make wrong use of the authority of the apostles. But for conserving the Gospel of Christ for all ages (in the New Testament) the dignity and authority given by Jesus to His apostles as His representatives on earth were of the utmost importance.

The clear teaching of the Fourth Gospel

Although the term "$ἀπόστολοι$" is never applied to the Twelve in the Fourth Gospel it is pre-eminently in this Gospel that we see how deliberately our Lord before His death prepared the disciples for the time, so close at hand, when they would not have Him in His bodily presence with them and would have to go into the world as His $ἀπόστολοι$. Of especial significance here is His promise to send to them the Holy spirit, the $παράκλητος$, who will give them all the necessary equipment for their high but extremely difficult and dangerous calling: "These things have I spoken unto you, while yet abiding with you. But the Paraclete, the Holy Spirit, whom the Father will send ($πέμψει$) in my name, he shall teach you all things, and bring to your remembrance all that I said unto you" (John xiv. 25 f.) Thus our Lord promises them that through the enlightening work of the Holy Ghost they will be enabled to remember and understand the significance of His teachings and of all truth pertaining to Him so that they will be able to perform their commission to teach others as His representatives. And in verse 12 He gave them the assurance that they would receive all the necessary power to act as His "apostles": "Verily, verily, I say unto you, He that believeth on me, the works that I do shall he do also; and greater works shall he do; because I go unto the Father." He also made it clear that, although He was going to leave them, He would come back in and through the Spirit to be with them always (John xiv. 18, 23).

In xvi. 12–14 our Lord clearly teaches them that they are as yet not at all prepared for the task to act as His "apostles", but He promises that they will soon be fully equipped: "I have yet many things to say unto you, but ye cannot bear them now. Howbeit when he, the Spirit of truth, is come, he shall guide you into all truth: for he shall not speak from himself: but what things soever he shall hear, these shall he speak: and he shall declare unto you things that are to come [the promise that they will be given the gift of prophetic insight]. He shall glorify me: for he shall take of mine, and shall declare it unto you."

In this Jesus thus promises that through the Holy Spirit they will be enabled to understand the whole truth concerning Him —be led fully into the mysteries of the kingdom, so that they may be able to witness correctly concerning Him and represent Him in an adequate manner.

After the resurrection

After His resurrection our Lord still more explicitly commissioned the apostles to be His שְׁלוּחִים, as John xx. 21 ff. shows: "Jesus therefore said to them again, Peace be unto you: as the Father hath sent me, even so send I you. And when he had said this, he breathed on them, and saith unto them, Receive ye the Holy Ghost: whose soever sins ye forgive, they are forgiven unto them; whose soever sins ye retain, they are retained."

Another important fact is that stated in Luke xxiv. 45: "Then opened he their mind, that they might understand the scriptures." This proved to be one of the most important factors in their equipment to act as His "apostles", for in the fulfilment of their commission the Old Testament, as the authoritative word of God which Christ came to fulfil, played a basic *rôle*.

Our Lord after the resurrection reiterated also the promise that through the Holy Ghost they would be equipped for their calling as His שְׁלוּחִים. Behold, I send forth the promise of my Father upon you: but tarry ye in the city, until ye be clothed with power from on high" (Luke xxiv. 49). "Ye shall receive power, when the Holy Ghost is come upon you: and ye shall be my witnesses. . . ." (Acts i. 8).

It is significant that in Matthew xxviii. 18 ff., where our Lord finally commissioned the disciples to go into the world as His apostles, He first said: "All authority [ἐξουσία] hath been given unto me in heaven and on earth", and then says: "Go therefore, and make disciples of all the nations. . . ." Because He is the Lord of all authority He can send them out to act in His name and for His sake to the glory of the Father. These words are undoubtedly meant also for all believers; nevertheless they were addressed in a special sense to His apostles, for in Acts i. 2 we read: "until the day in which he was received up, after that he had given commandment through the Holy Ghost unto the apostles whom he had chosen: to whom he also presented himself alive after his passion by many proofs, appearing unto them by the space of forty days, and speaking the things concerning the kingdom of God." From this it is clear that our Lord primarily directed Himself to His chosen apostles during the days between His resurrection and ascension—preparing them to act as His authoritative representatives through whom He was to lay the foundations of His Church.

Paul, the apostle to the gentiles, called by the Lord Himself

After the powerful beginning of the Church at Pentecost, it was, under the leadership of the twelve apostles, spreading rapidly through the Jewish world and even beyond the boundaries of Palestine (Acts viii.). It was, however, founded by the Lord to become His world-wide ἐκκλησία. And now the Heavenly King of the Church appears to Saul of Tarsus, who, still "breathing threatening and slaughter against the disciples of the Lord" (Acts ix. 1), is on his way to Damascus as a שָׁלִיחַ of the Jewish rulers—clothed with their authority to act against believers of Jewish descent in that city. And thus is called the "apostle to the gentiles" who is soon to become the man in whom the apostleship found its classic expression. Through the power of the Living Saviour the persecuting Jewish שָׁלִיחַ is changed to the ἀπόστολος κατ' ἐξοχήν of Him to whom is given all authority in heaven and on earth (Matt. xxviii. 18).

Just as in the case of the original apostles, it is again Jesus Himself who calls, equips and sends forth the "apostle to the gentiles". This comes out clearly in the history of Paul's meeting with the living Lord. "And it came to pass, that, as I made my journey, and drew nigh unto Damascus, about noon, suddenly there shone from heaven a great light round about me. And I fell unto the ground and heard a voice saying unto me, Saul, Saul, why persecutest thou me? And I answered, Who art thou, Lord? And he said unto me, I am Jesus of Nazareth, whom thou persecutest. . . . And I said, What shall I do, Lord? And the Lord said unto me, Arise, and go into Damascus, and there it shall be told thee of all things which are appointed for thee to do" (Acts xxii. 6–10), "for to this end have I appeared unto thee, to appoint thee a minister and a witness both of the things wherein thou hast seen me, and of the things wherein I will appear unto thee; delivering thee from the people, and from the gentiles unto whom I send [$\dot{\alpha}\pi o\sigma\tau\acute{\epsilon}\lambda\lambda\omega$] thee" (Acts xxvi. 16 f.).

From this it appears clearly how the Sovereign Lord Himself changed, called and appointed Paul to be His "apostle" in the fullest sense of the word—one clothed with the authority and endued with the power of his Sender, to go forth and act as His representative in the fulfilling of the commission given to him. For everyone who does not accept the historicity of this, the life of Paul will always be an unsolved riddle. Only on the basis of the actual fact of his call and commission by the Divine Lord can we understand why Paul afterwards acted with such uncompromising authority as the apostle of Jesus Christ.[1]

Given the gift of the Holy Spirit

Apart from revealing Himself as Saviour and Lord to Paul and explicitly appointing him to be His apostle, our Lord gave to him

[1] Rengstorf declares rightly that is it indubitably certain that "das Apostolatsbewüsztsein des Paulus ganz wesentlich durch seine Begegnung mit Jesus bei Damaskus bestimmt ist" (the consciousness of Paul of being an Apostle was in a very real sense determined by his encounter with Jesus near Damascus) (*op. cit.*, p. 439).

also in a very special way the gift of the Holy Spirit to equip him for his task. For Ananias of Damascus, sent by Him, "entered into the house [where the blinded Paul was]; and laying his hands on him said, Brother Saul, the Lord, even Jesus, who appeared unto thee in the way which thou camest, hath sent me, that thou mayest receive thy sight, and be filled with the Holy Ghost" (Acts ix. 17). Endued with power from on high, changed completely from the Jewish שָׁלִיחַ to the apostle of Christ, "straightway in the synagogues he proclaimed Jesus that he is the Son of God" (Acts ix. 20). And throughout the greater part of the rest of the book of Acts we see how the exalted Lord, through the mighty working of His Spirit, continually enabled Paul, amid all circumstances, to act as His ἀπόστολος in His name, on His authority and through His power. And, just as in the case of the original apostles, the Lord gave the visible vindication of His apostle's authority through the miraculous deeds he was enabled to perform in the name of Jesus, but above all through the astounding success of his missionary labours. So what is said of the original apostles in Mark xvi. 20 applies fully also to the "apostle to the gentiles"; namely, "they went forth, and preached everywhere, the Lord working with them, and confirming the word by the signs that followed".

II

THE APOSTLES THEMSELVES CLAIMED TO POSSESS AND EXERCISED AUTHORITY

HAVING seen how Jesus, the King and Lord of His Church, called, prepared, equipped and sent forth His apostles as men clothed with His authority, and how He confirmed their authority, let us now turn to the apostles themselves as they are presented to us in Acts and the rest of the New Testament.

Immediately we find that they were supremely conscious of the fact that they had been sent as the שְׁלוּחִים of their exalted Lord, and that they consistently claimed to possess and exercised the unique authority with which only actual apostles of Christ could be clothed.

Ten days after the ascension the promise of the Lord to send the Holy Ghost is fulfilled and immediately the apostles, who were a few weeks before so weak and helpless, are changed to men who have manifestly become the "apostles" of the risen Lord. In Acts ii. 14 (after verses 12 and 13 related how some from the multitudes were amazed at the Pentecost phenomena and others were mocking) it is stated: "But Peter, standing up with the eleven [Mathias had been chosen in Judas' place—i. 21 f.], lifted up his voice, and spoke forth unto them. . . ."

From that moment things begin to move with tremendous power, and throughout the first eight chapters of Acts we see the apostles[1]

---

[1] Harnack, great as he is as a scholar, propounded remarkably fantastic ideas concerning the origin of the view held in the Early Church that the original apostles possessed such great authority. The main tenets of his theory are that the Lord (to whom Harnack does not ascribe the absolute divine authority the New Testament does) appointed the Twelve to be His *disciples* (not apostles) and that they had influence practically only in the Jerusalem Church. There they were waiting for the Messiah to return and elevate them to rulers in the Messianic

acting as the fully authorized representatives of their Sender, Christ Jesus the Lord. They "preach Christ" (Acts viii. 5, 35) (not His teachings, or their own theories and philosophies, but Himself)

kingdom. But in his missionary journeys "Paul put them in front (as *apostles*); in order to set the dignity of his own office in its true light, he embraced the Twelve under the category of the *original apostolate* (thereby allowing their personal discipleship to fall into the background, in his terminology), and thus raised them above all other apostles, although not higher than the level which he claimed to occupy himself. That the Twelve henceforth rank in history as the twelve apostles, and in fact as *the* apostles, was a result brought about by Paul; and paradoxically enough, this was brought about by him in his efforts to fix the value of his own apostleship" (*Expansion of Christianity*, Eng. trans., New York, 1904, i, p. 403). How utterly in conflict with the actual facts such ideas are has already appeared from what we have discussed, and even in his own writings Harnack contradicts himself regarding this matter. Cf., for instance, his statement that "the Church at Jerusalem, together with the primitive apostles, considered themselves the central body of Christendom, and also the representatives of the true Israel" (*ibid.*, p. 413). Cf. also his admission that at least Peter of the original apostles acted as a real apostle just as Paul (*ibid.*, p. 441).

In his *Lehrbuch der Dogmengeschichte*, i, pp. 180 f., he has an entirely different theory as to why the twelve apostles were elevated to such a place of authority. Having called the belief in the supreme significance of the Twelve a "dogmatischen Geschichtsconstruction" (p. 180) he has the following fantastic argumentation: "In den Gemeinden, welche Paulus gestiftet und längere Zeit hindurch geleitet hatte, muss das Gedächtnis an die Controversen des apostolischen Zeitalters sehr bald erloschen und das Vacuum, welches so entstand, durch eine Theorie ausgefüllt worden sein, die den status quo in den heidenchristlichen Gemeinden direct auf eine ihn begründende Ueberliéferung der Zwölf zurück führte" (In the congregations which Paul had founded and had led throughout for a considerable time, the remembrance of the controversies of the apostolic era must very soon have been effaced and the vacuum that originated in this way must have been filled up by a theory that carried back the *status quo* in the Gentile-Christian congregations directly to a tradition of the Twelve confirming it) (*ibid.*). Thus, whereas in the statements quoted above from another writing of his, he says Paul was responsible for having elevated the twelve *disciples* of Jesus to the twelve authoritative apostles, he here pictures Paul as one who had been engaged in prolonged controversies with the original apostles and that it was the gentile Churches who "filled the vacuum" (after the memories of the controversies had subsided) by fabricating the idea of the authority of the primitive apostles. No wonder that Harnack himself declared concerning this supposed development: "Diese Thatsache ist ausserordentlich paradox" (This fact is exceptionally paradoxical) (*ibid.*). If he accepted the witness of the New Testament and of the Early Church regarding the authority of the apostles, he would have seen how the different real facts fitted into each other, and would not have had to try (so in vain) to give explanations to his self-made paradoxes.

with power. And thousands of people come to believe in Jesus, receiving forgiveness of sins and eternal salvation (Acts ii. 37-42, 47, iv. 33). And thus began to be fulfilled our Lord's promise to Peter that he, and with him the other apostles, would be the rock on which His Church would be built, that through them He would begin His Church, and bring men to the experience of the forgiveness of sins.

So obvious were the signs[1] that pointed to the fact that the apostles acted with authority that even the Jewish rulers could not help perceiving it. "Now when they beheld the boldness of Peter and John, and had perceived that they were unlearned and ignorant men, they marvelled; and they took knowledge of them, that they had been with Jesus" (Acts iv. 13).

Their authority vindicated

Not only did the apostles preach and teach with manifest authority but they also acted with authority in guiding the life of the Church in those early days. And their authority was vindicated by the signs and wonders they performed in the name and through the power of their Lord. "In the name of Jesus Christ of Nazareth, walk," said Peter to the lame man at the temple. "And he took him by the right hand, and raised him up: and immediately his feet and anklebones received strength" (Acts iii. 6 f.). To Ananias, who tried to deceive, Peter said: "why hath Satan filled thy heart to lie to the Holy Ghost?" and both he and his wife died at the feet of the apostle without any human intervention (v. 1-6). On the other hand, Peter healed the bedridden Æneas (ix. 34) and raised the dead Tabitha to life again (ix. 40). Luke only mentions a few examples out of many more; for in v. 12 he states: "by the hands of the apostles were many signs and wonders wrought among the people."

[1] These signs done by the apostles also belong, to use Rengstorf's words, "zum Wesen der Dinge, da in ihr der Bote selbst den Erweis hat und liefert, dasz er wirklich Jesu Beauftragter ist und ihn vertritt" (to the essence of things, because in it the messenger himself has and furnishes the proof that he is really Jesus' deputy and represents Him) (*op. cit.*, p. 430).

Thus our Lord's promise that the apostles would be fully equipped and empowered for their task was in every way fulfilled. So they who had previously been disciples ($\mu\alpha\theta\eta\tau\alpha\iota$ = followers and learners) had become in the highest sense שְׁלוּחִים, teaching and acting on the authority and through the power of the Spirit of their living Lord. And it is significant that the Twelve are never called disciples in Acts but consistently "apostles".[1]

The apostles in Acts

It has often been said regarding the second book of Luke that the title "The Acts of the Apostles" is an inappropriate title for this book, and that it should rather have been called "The Acts of the Holy Spirit" or "The Acts of the Risen Lord". There is much truth in this, because in final reality everything in the beginning and development of the Church as described in Acts is the work of the Lord of the Church through His Spirit. But the indisputable fact remains that throughout Acts we see God in Christ moving in history not independent of but through the instrumentality of the

---

[1] How inconsistent with the real facts is Harnack's theory that the apostles were only at a later date elevated by Paul and other missionaries to men of such supreme authority! Cf. his words: "And so now appeared that strange phenomenon—the 'twelve apostles' as the court of highest instance and of fundamental authority. Soon also the belief took shape that Christ had committed the continuation and expansion of His work to the twelve once for all, and so completely that every real mission is subordinate to them and receives from them its content and authority. . . . Since the end of the first century the apostles already seemed to the Gentile Church like a multiplication of the Christ. . . . What Serapion says at the beginning of the third century (Eusebius, H.E. vi. 12, 3): ἡμεῖς καὶ πέτρον καὶ τοὺς ἄλλους ἀποστόλους ἀποδεχόμεθα ὡς χριστον could certainly also have been said a hundred years earlier" (*Origin of the New Testament*, pp. 47 f.).

What Harnack says in the last two sentences concerning the situation in the Early Church is exactly what we found to be the actual truth. The apostles *were* looked upon as clothed with the authority of the Lord in such a unique way. But he moves entirely outside all available evidence where he declares that this belief in the ἐξουσία of the apostles was a later creation of the Church. As we have sufficiently clearly seen, their authority is based on the fact that the Lord Himself called, equipped and sent them forth as His apostles and enabled them to act as such, especially after Pentecost.

apostles, first of the Twelve and then of Paul. Very seldom do other Christian leaders such as Philip and Barnabas appear in the picture. It is consistently the especially chosen and authoritative שְׁלוּחִים of Christ the Lord who are shown to us in this book as the men in and through whom Jesus wrought mightily in the laying, for all times, of the foundations of the Church.

But let us now proceed to the New Testament epistles to hear what they declare about the authority of the apostles of the Lord.

Emphatic claims by Paul

One of the most outstanding facts concerning the epistles of the Apostle Paul is that in nearly every one of them he emphatically claims that he is an apostle of the Lord. For instance, he begins his epistle to the Romans with the words: "Paul, a bondservant of Jesus Christ, called to be an apostle [שָׁלַח]." 1 Corinthians i. 1 reads: "Paul, called to be an apostle of Jesus Christ." And Galatians i. 1 puts it even more emphatically: "Paul, an apostle (not from men, neither through men, but through Jesus Christ, and God the Father. . . .)."

That Paul knew what the real significance was of being an ἀπόστολος follows already from the fact that before his conversion he was accustomed to be sent by the Jewish rulers as a שָׁלַח to act in their name and on their authority. But apart from this, there are many indications in his letters that he not only knew that he was called and commissioned by Christ to be His apostle in the fullest sense, but also realized the implications of this fact. As we proceed with our discussion we shall see the evidence for this. At this point we merely wish to draw attention to the following significant fact: where at the beginning of his letters he mentions another person or persons as joint-authors, he explicitly declares that only he is an apostle and the others merely believers. So Colossians i. 1 reads: "Paul, an apostle of Christ Jesus . . . and Timothy, the brother." 2 Corinthians i. 1 has the same words, emphasizing the fact that whereas Paul is an apostle Timothy is only a "brother". And

Galatians i. 1 has: "Paul the apostle. . . . And all the brethren which are with me." Not in a single case does the apostle call his companions "apostles" in the opening words of his letters. On the other hand, he clearly recognizes and proclaims the fact that the original apostles of the Lord are legitimately so called, as they, too, had been chosen and commissioned by Jesus Himself. So Galatians ii. 8 reads: "he that wrought for Peter unto the apostleship of the circumcision wrought for me also unto the Gentiles" (cf. also 1 Cor. xv. 1–16).

Only in four places does Paul use the word ἀπόστολος in connection with persons other than himself and the original Twelve. In 2 Corinthians viii. 23 he speaks of "our brethren, the apostles of the churches". Thus he clearly states that they are not apostles of the Lord but are ordinary "brethren" who have been commissioned by the Churches to do missionary work and are only for this reason called "apostles". In Philippians ii. 25 we have a similar case. For here Paul says of Epaphroditus that he is "your apostle and minister to my need". He is thus merely one sent to act in the name of and as the representative of the Church of Philippi. This has accordingly nothing to do with being an apostle (שָׁלִיַח) of the Lord. And it is significant that while Paul in these two cases speaks of men being apostles of Churches, he never speaks of himself or of the original apostles being ἀπόστολοι of Churches, but always stresses the fact that they are the called שְׁלוּחִים of the Sovereign Lord.

In Romans xvi. 7 Paul says of Andronicus and Junias that they are "of note among the apostles". Some take it as meaning that Andronicus and Junias were noted *as apostles*. Others again say Paul meant that the apostles had high regard for these two believers. Exegetes differ in the interpretation of this verse. But in any case, in the light of Paul's consistent attitude regarding the apostleship as we have seen above, it seems to me entirely illegitimate to take this casual remark of the apostle as proving that he recognized persons other than himself and the original Twelve (Matthias being in the place of Judas) as being, in the highest sense of the words, apostles of the Lord.¹ The only exception might be James, the brother of Jesus (Gal. i. 19). But even here it is not quite² sure that Paul declared that he is a שָׁלִיחַ of the Lord. If Galatians i. 19, however, does mean this, it can be understood in the light of the fact that, as Paul himself states in 1 Corinthians xv. 7, the risen Saviour after the resurrection appeared in a very special way to James. And the fact that James played such a leading role in the Early Church may perhaps indicate that our Lord called and commissioned him to be an extraordinary "apostle" of His.³

Only the original apostles and Paul

Taking everything into consideration, all available evidence⁴ points overwhelmingly to the fact that, *in the highest sense of the word, only the original apostles and Paul were called and appointed to*

---

¹ If he meant that Andronicus and Junias are "apostles", he must, seen in the light of his other statements, have meant it in the wider sense of authorized missionaries of the Church. Cf. Acts xiv. 4, where Paul and Barnabas are called "apostles" in the sense of being authorized missionaries of the Church at Antioch.

² Even J. B. Lightfoot, who pleads very strongly for the ascribing of apostleship to James, can only say that in Galatians i. 19 he is "apparently so entitled" (*Epistle to the Galatians*, London, 1865, p. 92, n. 4), and of 1 Corinthians xv. 7 he can also just say St. Paul "appears to include James among the apostles" (*ibid.*).

³ The argument is often used (cf. Harnack, *Expansion of Christianity*, i. p. 402) that passages like 2 Corinthians xi. 13 and Revelation ii. 2, speaking of "false apostles", show that the apostleship (in highest sense) was not limited to Paul and the Twelve. This is surely a precarious argument. For although the Twelve and Paul were made the apostles of the Lord by the Lord, it does not mean that everyone in the Church, and especially the "heretically minded" people, would accept their authority in an automatic way. It is quite natural that some unruly or misguided persons would present themselves as the real bearers of the truth and so as "apostles of the Lord", and could then be referred to as "false apostles".

⁴ We must, however, also remember that is was "after the murder of James the son of Zebedee that James the Lord's brother comes on the scene. He may have taken the place of his namesake in the number of the Twelve" (Alfred Plummer, *op. cit.*, p. 83). It seems very natural to suppose that just as previously under divine guidance they chose Matthias to fill the place of Judas, they did the same with James after the comparatively early death of his namesake.

be the שְׁלוּחִים of the exalted Lord.[1] Where Barnabas is called an apostle in Acts xiv. 4, 14, it is clearly only in the sense of one being sent by the Church as a fully commissioned missionary but not as an ἀπόστολος τοῦ χριστοῦ (cf. Acts xiii, xiv) in the highest sense as used of the Twelve and Paul.[2]

To bring out still more clearly the fact that the original apostles as well as Paul claimed that they were chosen and equipped in a unique way to be the only שְׁלוּחִים of Christ, let us turn to Acts x. 39 ff., where Peter says in the name of the Twelve: "we are witnesses of all things which he [Jesus] did both in the country of the Jews, and in Jerusalem. ... Him God raised up the third day, and gave him to be manifest, not to all the people, but unto the witnesses that were chosen before of God, even to us, who did eat and drink with him after he arose from the dead. And he charged us to preach unto the people, and to testify. ..."

That not merely the fact that someone had been with Jesus and had seen Him after His resurrection elevated him to the position of apostle appears clearly from Acts i. 21-6, where the appointment

[1] Apostleship in its highest sense as applied to the Twelve and Paul was, to use Rengstorf's words, "kein Gemeindeamt, geschweige 'denn 'das vornehmste', sondern das Amt Jesu, das die Kirche baut" (no congregational office, to say nothing of "the most important", but the office of Jesus that builds the Church) (*op. cit.*, p. 423).

[2] J. B. Lightfoot writes that Paul in the Galatian letter "speaks of Barnabas as associated with himself in the apostleship of the Gentiles (ii. 9)" (*Epistle to the Galatians*, p. 93). But there seems to me no reason for saying this, because Paul says explicitly in the previous verse (Gal. ii. 8) that God wrought for him (Paul) unto the apostleship of the Gentiles. He does not mention Barnabas at all in this verse, and in the following verse he is not speaking of the apostleship from God but of the hand of friendship extended to him and Barnabas by Peter and the others. These verses thus show how Paul looked upon his apostleship as so unique that only the apostleship of the Twelve can be placed on the same level with his (cf. ii. 8 (a)). The statement of Lightfoot that "in the First to the Corinthians Paul claims for (Barnabas) his fellow-labourer all the privileges of an apostle, as one who like himself holds the office of an apostle and is doing the work of an apostle (ix. 5)" (*ibid.*) is also ungrounded. For in ix. 1 f., where he speaks of his apostleship in explicit terms, he again mentions only himself, and only afterwards, when he discusses practical matters, he names Barnabas. Paul certainly looked upon Barnabas as an important missionary of the Church, but nowhere ascribes to him the same form of apostleship that he and the Twelve were appointed to.

of someone to fill the place of Judas is described. Peter, addressing the brethren, said: "Of the men therefore which have accompanied with us all the time that the Lord Jesus went in and went out among us, beginning from the baptism of John, unto the day that he was received up from us, of these must one become a witness with us of his resurrection. And they put forward two, Joseph called Barsabbas, who was surnamed Justus, and Matthias. And they prayed, and said, Thou, Lord, which knowest the hearts of all men, shew of these two the one whom thou hast chosen, to take the place in this ministry and apostleship."

Let us now compare the words of Paul in Galatians i. 1: "Paul, an apostle (not from men, neither through men, but through Jesus Christ, and God the Father. . . .)." Compare also 1 Timothy ii. 7, where he says of the Gospel: "whereunto I was appointed a herald and an apostle (I speak the truth, I lie not)." In 1 Corinthians ix. 1 he exclaims: "am I not an apostle? have I not seen Jesus our Lord?" And in 1 Corinthians xv. 8–10, after having related the appearances of our Lord to the original apostles, to the five hundred brethren and to James, he says: "and last of all, as unto one born out of due time, he appeared[1] to me also. For I am the least of the apostles, that am not meet to be called an apostle, because I persecuted the church of God. But by the grace of God I am what I am . . ."

The basis of their claim

From all of this it is clear on what the apostles based their claim that they, and they alone, are the שְׁלוּחִים of the Lord; namely, they saw the risen Jesus and He Himself chose, commissioned

---

[1] J. B. Lightfoot has said: "If, therefore, St. Paul has held a larger place than Barnabas in the gratitude and veneration of the Church of all ages, this is due not to any superiority of rank or office, but to the ascendancy of his personal gifts, a more intense energy and self-devotion, wider and deeper sympathies, a firmer intellectual grasp, a larger measure of the Spirit of Christ" (*op. cit.*, p. 93). Although there is some element of truth in this, he leaves out the most important fact of all; namely, that the Living Lord in a very special way appeared to Paul on the way to Damascus and called and equipped him to be the apostle to the Gentiles κατ' ἐξοχήν. These facts place Paul on a completely different plane than Barnabas and his other fellow-workers (except Peter and the rest of the Twelve).

and equipped them to be His "apostles". The original apostles had the additional qualification that they had been with Jesus throughout His public ministry.[1] But in the case of Paul this lack had been made good by the very special way in which the Lord appeared to him and by the fact that He gave him exceptional grace and power to fulfil his calling (1 Cor. xv. 10).

Never again could or can there be persons who possess all these qualifications to be the שְׁלוּחִים of Jesus. Just as the revelation of God in Christ is ἐφαπαξ, "einmalig" (once for all), the action of the risen Lord in and through His apostles in laying the foundations of His Church for all time is once for all.[2]

That the apostles were conscious of this appears from the whole history in Acts and from many declarations in the Epistles, such as the following. In Ephesians ii. 20 Paul speaks of the Church "being built upon the foundation of the apostles and prophets, Christ Jesus himself being the chief corner stone". In 2 Corinthians

[1] In the light of the New Testament teaching "scheint neben der Begegnung mit dem Auferstandenen der persönliche Auftrag von ihm der alleinige Grund des Apostolats gewesen zu sein. Dasz dieser Auftrag vor allem den Zwölf galt, liegt in ihrem Anteil an der Geschichte des irdischen Jesus beschlossen, der sie in besonderer Weise geeignet macht, seine Verkündigung wieder aufzunehmen und fortzuführen" (it seems that, next to meeting with the arisen One, the commission from Him had been the only ground of the apostolate. That this commission above all concerned the Twelve is comprised in their share in the history of the earthly Jesus, that makes them in a special manner capable of again taking up and carrying forward His preaching) (Rengstorf, *op. cit.*, p. 432).

[2] It is at this point important to remember also the facts mentioned by Alfred Plummer in the following: "The absence from Christ's teaching of any statement respecting the priesthood of the Twelve, or respecting the transmission of the powers of the Twelve to others, is remarkable. As the primary function of the Twelve was to be witnesses of what Christ had taught and done, especially in rising from the dead, no transmission of so exceptional an office was possible. Even with regard to the high authority which all apostles possessed, it is not clear that it was a jurisdiction which was to be passed on from generation to generation. . . . The apostles were commissioned to found a living Church, with power to supply itself with ministers and to organize them" (*op. cit.*, p. 84). Rengstorf says in this connection, respecting the character of the apostleship: "darum ist es weiter nur folgerichtig, wenn der Apostolat auf die erste Generation beschränkt geblieben und nicht zu einem kirchlichen Amt geworden ist" (therefore it is moreover only logically correct, if the apostolate remained limited to the first generation and did not become an ecclesiastical office) (*op. cit.*, p. 433).

xi. 1–15 he says "the truth of Christ is in me" and declares that those who preach a different gospel than he preached "are false apostles, deceitful workers, fashioning themselves into apostles of Christ. And no marvel; for even Satan fashioneth himself into an angel of light. It is no great thing therefore if his ministers also fashion themselves as ministers of righteousness" (2 Cor. xi. 13–15). And we all know those impassioned words of his in Galatians i. 8, 11: "though we, or an angel from heaven, should preach unto you any gospel other than that which we preached unto you, let him be anathema.... For I make known to you, brethren, as touching the gospel which was preached by me, that it is not after man. For neither did I receive it from man, nor was I taught it, but it came to me through revelation of Jesus Christ." A little further on he has the words: "it was the good pleasure of God, who separated me, even from my mother's womb, and called me through his grace, to reveal his Son in me, that I might preach him...." (1–15, 16).

Paul thus unequivocally declares that the preaching of the Gospel by him and the other apostles has an ἐφαπαξ, once-for-all character, because Christ Jesus Himself gave them the authority and the equipment to act and teach as His שְׁלוּחִם.

Peter and John

Also in the epistles of Peter and John the same claims are made that they are writing as men having the authority and equipment to write. 1 Peter i. 1 reads: "Peter, an apostle of Jesus Christ", and 2 Peter i. 1: "Simon Peter, a servant and apostle of Jesus Christ." In another form the same authority is claimed in 1 John i. 1–5: "That which was from the beginning, that which we have heard, that which we have seen with our eyes, that which we beheld, and our hands handled, concerning the Word of life (and the life was manifested, and we have seen, and bear witness, and declare unto you the life, the eternal life, which was with the Father, and was manifested unto us); that which we have seen and heard declare we unto you also.... And this is the message which we have heard from him, and announce unto you...."

And the fact that the apostles were called to lay the foundation of the Church is described in pictorial form in Revelation xxi. 14, where it is said of the new Jerusalem: "And the wall of the city had twelve foundations, and on them twelve names of the twelve apostles of the Lamb."[1]

The first place given to the apostles

The fundamental importance of the apostles in laying the foundations, or rather of being used by Christ to lay the foundations of His Church, is brought out clearly also by the way Paul, in naming the different groups of leaders in the Church of those days, always names the apostles first. "He gave some to be apostles; and some prophets . . ." (Eph. iv. 11). In 1 Corinthians xii. 28 he makes it even more explicit by saying: "God hath set in the church, first apostles, secondly prophets. . . ." And this is in fullest harmony with the history described in Acts. For there we see how, in regulating Church matters and in preaching Christ, the apostles are the supreme leaders, whereas the prophets appear only occasionally, and then solely to give some special warning that was needed at a particular point of time regarding some or other practical matter.

All our evidence thus shows the untenableness of the view of Harnack[2] (*The Origin of the New Testament*, London, 1925, pp. 20 ff.) that the charismatic "bearers of the Spirit" above all, and the apostles only in so far as they were also "bearers of the Spirit", were the supreme authorities and leaders of the Early Church and not the apostles as the only שְׁלוּחִים of the Lord. L. Leipoldt (*Geschischte*

[1] J. B. Lightfoot has rightly declared: "The 'twelve apostles of the Lamb' in the figurative language of St. John represent the whole apostolate . . ." (*Epistle to the Galatians*, p. 92).

[2] Speaking of the persons of authority in the Early Church, he declares: "in primitive Christendom, though every Christian was believed to have received the Spirit, certain members were regarded as being specially inspired, as being 'bearers of the Spirit' κατ'ἐξοχήν. The directions of these 'apostles, prophets and teachers' could not but be simply accepted and obeyed . . . if they gave any directions concerning written works, these also could not but be obeyed. In these 'bearers of the Spirit' the Churches thus possessed, until far into the second century, authorities that could create that what was *new* and could give to the new the seal of prescription" (p. 20).

SUPREME AUTHORITY 77

des neutest Kanons, vol. i, 1907, p. 33) to a large extent follows Harnack and declares, for instance: "tatsächlich bildeten die urchristlichen Apokalypsen den Grundstock eines neutestamentlichen Kanons" (actually the early Christian "apocalypses" formed the pedestal of a New Testament canon).

There is, as we have already seen, absolutely no real evidence in the New Testament for these views of Harnack *cum suis*, and, as we shall presently see, the witness of the early Fathers is in complete accord with the New Testament in this matter.

The apostles acted with authority

In order to fulfil their task in laying the foundations of the Church as the authorized שְׁלוּחִים of the Lord of the Church, it was necessary that the apostles should act with authority in regulating the life of the Church according to the will of their Sender. And again we find, both in Acts and the Epistles, that the apostles not only claimed to possess the authority to do this, but actually put their God-given ἐξουσία into effect. We have already pointed out how much evidence for this there is in Acts, and here only wish to refer to Acts vi. 2 ff. as showing the authoritative way in which the apostles acted. For we read there: "the twelve called the multitude of the disciples unto them, and said, It is not fit that we should forsake the word of God, and serve the tables. Look ye out therefore, brethren, from among you seven men of good report, full of the Spirit and of wisdom, whom *we* [my italics] may appoint over this business... they chose Stephen... whom they sat before the apostles: and when they had prayed, they laid their hands on them." The same fact appears in viii. 14 ff. "Now when the apostles which were at Jerusalem heard that Samaria had received the word of God, they sent unto them Peter and John, who, when they were come down, prayed for them, that they might receive the Holy Ghost.... Then laid they their hands on them and they received the Holy Ghost." Throughout the first twelve chapters of Acts we see how the Lord through His Spirit used pre-eminently the apostles as His שְׁלוּחִים to build His Church, and in the rest of Acts we see how Paul as the chosen apostle is used in a similar way in the founding and building of the Church in much wider areas.

When we turn to his epistles we find once more in what wonderful harmony his own statements in this matter are with the picture of the facts given in Acts. His words in 2 Thessalonians iii. 4, 6 are typical of many of his declarations, showing how he acted as one clothed with the authority of his Lord.[1] For after having said, in verse 4, "we have confidence in the Lord touching you, that ye both do and will do the things which we command", he goes on to say, in verse 6: "Now we command[2] you, brethren, in the name of our Lord Jesus Christ...." The same claim to possess authority to give orders to the Churches in the name of the King of the Church appears in words of his like the following: "For though I should glory somewhat abundantly concerning our authority (which the Lord gave . . .) I shall not be put to shame" (2 Cor. x. 8). In 2 Corinthians xiii. 10 he says: "For this cause I write these things while absent, that I may not when present deal sharply, according to the authority [ἐξουσία] which the Lord gave me...." Compare

[1] Paul acted so consciously as the apostle of the Lord that in his letters "sie zurückweisen heiszt den Herrn zurückweisen; ihnen widersprechen heiszt dem Evangelium widersprechen; sie sind die authentischen Interpreten der vollkommenen Offenbarung Gottes in Christo" (to repulse them means to repulse the Lord; to contradict them means to contradict the Gospel; they are the authentic interpreters of the perfect revelation of God in Christ) (Jülicher-Fascher, op. cit., p. 462).

[2] Contrast with this the way in which the Apostolic Fathers wrote (see our next section on "The Authority of the Apostles was acknowledged in the Early Church"). Nowhere in the early Christian writings outside the New Testament do we find anything so explicit as the way in which Paul claimed supreme God-given authority. An apparent exception is the words in I Clement, par. 63: "For ye will give us great joy and gladness, if ye render obedience unto the things written by us through the Holy Spirit, and root out the unrighteous anger of your jealousy, according to the entreaty which we have made for peace and concord in this letter." That this is, however, entirely different from Paul's way of writing with apostolic authority follows from the following facts: (1) the letter is written in the name (not of Clement) but of the Church at Rome; (2) from beginning to end the letter unreservedly accepts the final authority of Paul and the original apostles (cf. pars. 5 and 42); (3) even in the sentence just preceding the quoted verse the letter speaks of the submission of the Christians in Rome themselves to the "leaders of our souls"; (4) the letter speaks of "entreaty" but not of a "command".

also 1 Corinthians iv. 21. Note, too, especially what he says in 1 Corinthians v. 3 ff.: "For I verily, being absent in body but present in spirit, have already, as though I were present, judged him [the sinner] that hath so wrought this thing, in the name of our Lord Jesus, ye being gathered together, and my spirit, with the power of our Lord Jesus, to deliver such a one unto Satan for the destruction of the flesh, that the spirit may be saved in the day of the Lord Jesus."

Who else than one supremely conscious of the fact that to him has been given divine authority in the Church could speak in this way? We seek in vain for anything similar in the writings of the Early Church Fathers.

It is therefore abundantly clear how untenable Manson's view[1] is that Paul looked upon "apostles" as meaning "missionaries" and not as "authoritative representatives" (men to whom our Lord gave supreme dignity and authority as His שְׁלוּחִים). What Manson stresses, namely that the apostles were called to "the beneficent activity which overcomes evil by redeeming the sinners from the thraldom of the kingdom of Satan into the service and freedom of the Kingdom of God",[2] is certainly true. But this is only one aspect of the significance of the apostles. And he is completely off the mark when he overlooks all the abundant evidence that points to the final authority given to the apostles. Paul would, in the light of the statements in his letters, certainly not have agreed with Manson!

Paul realized to such an extent that he is, together with the original apostles, an authoritative שָׁלִיחַ of the Lord, that he even holds forth himself as an example that must be followed. In 1 Corinthians xi. 1 he commands: "Be ye imitators of me, even as I also am of Christ"; and in 1 Corinthians iv. 15 ff. he writes: "in Christ Jesus I begat you through the gospel. I beseech you therefore, be ye imitators of me. For this cause have I sent unto you Timothy . . . who shall put you in remembrance of my ways in Christ, even as I teach everywhere in every church." In 1 Thessalonians i. 6 he touches upon the same matter by stating: "ye became imitators of us and of the Lord, having received the word. . . ."

[1] *Op. cit.*, pp. 241-3.   [2] *Ibid.*, p. 242.

Their authority vindicated

We have seen in Acts how God confirmed and vindicated the authority of the apostles of the Lord by enabling them to perform mighty deeds and above all by blessing their work as the representatives of Jesus in a manifest way. And this also is clearly reflected in the epistles of St. Paul. For in 2 Corinthians xii. 12 he declares: "Truly the signs of an apostle were wrought among you in all patience, by signs and wonders and mighty powers." In 1 Thessalonians i. 5 he writes: "Our gospel came not unto you in words only, but also in power, and in the Holy Ghost, and in much assurance." And in 1 Corinthians ix. 2 he writes of the large Corinthian Church which was mostly the fruit of his labours: "the seal of mine apostleship are ye in the Lord."

Their authority to teach

The most important aspect of the authority of the apostles is, however, their claim to possess, and their acting as men who do possess, the absolute $\dot{\epsilon}\xi ov\sigma i\alpha$ to teach the truth, the unadulterated Gospel of Christ. It has already become abundantly clear that in Acts both the original apostles and Paul are described as men who preached Jesus with authority. Turning to the Epistles we find the same fact consistently brought forward.

In 2 John x such an authority is claimed for the teaching of the Lord taught by the apostles that John declares: "If any one cometh unto you, and bringeth not this teaching, receive him not in your house, and give him no greeting." And Paul says of anyone that "preacheth another Jesus, whom we have not preached" (2 Cor. xi. 4) that he is a false apostle and a minister of Satan (verses 13 ff.).

In 1 Thessalonians ii. 13 he writes these remarkable words: "for this cause we also thank God without ceasing, that, when ye received from us the word of the message, even the word of God, ye accepted it not as the words of men, but as it is in truth, the word of God." Could he have expressed more explicitly the fact that he speaks on the authority, and in the name of Christ? The same truth is proclaimed by his words in Titus i. 3, where he says: God "in his own seasons manifested his words in the proclamation wherewith I was entrusted according to the commandment of God our Saviour".

We have already quoted in another connection those flaming words of Galatians i. 6–12, where Paul claimed in the most absolute terms to be an authorized preacher of the Gospel of Christ.

They did not theorize or speculate

There is no evidence in Acts or the Epistles that the authoritative apostles ever doubted the truth concerning Christ and His Gospel. In smaller practical details, especially concerning the terms of admission for the Gentiles, some of them did waver. But regarding the essential proclamation of the Gospel from beginning to end they spoke with power and authority. They did not theorize or speculate about matters, but proclaimed with unique assurance Jesus the Christ the Son of God. And this they were enabled to do, as they continually inform us, because Christ called them, made them His ambassadors (2 Cor. v. 20), and gave them all the necessary insight into the truth and the ability to proclaim it in an adequate way so that Paul could with fullest assurance declare to the elders of Ephesus that he had proclaimed to them "the whole counsel of God" (Acts xx. 27). This they did, not with worldly wisdom or through their own ability of attaining to truth, "But unto us God revealed it [the Gospel, the mystery of God] through the Spirit: for the Spirit searcheth all things, yea, the deep things of God . . . the things of God none knoweth, save the Spirit of God. But we received not the spirit of the world, but the Spirit which is of God: that we might know things that are freely given to us by God. Which things also we speak, not in words, which man's wisdom teacheth, but which the Spirit teacheth . . . we have the mind of Christ" (1 Cor. ii. 13–16).

So we see how gloriously the promise of our Lord in John xiv. 16 and xvi. 13, that He would send the Holy Spirit to guide the apostles into all truth and enable them to lay the permanent foundations of the Church, became fulfilled.¹

Authority claimed for written teachings too

Before ending our discussion a most important fact must still be named; namely, that pre-eminently the Apostle Paul claimed absolute authority not only for his oral teachings but also for his written epistles. This already follows from the fact that he so emphatically at the beginning of his letters declares that he is an apostle (שָׁלִיחַ) of Jesus Christ and of God the Father and thus claims to write in the Name and on the authority of God—so that his commands must be obeyed and his teachings accepted as true and authoritative.

But before showing that this is what Paul actually meant we must intercept a very common objection made to the statement that Paul claimed authority for his letters. Much is made, for example, of his words in 1 Corinthians vii. 10, 22, 25, 40, as if they showed that Paul wrote just as any Christian would do, giving his opinions according to the best of his insight, without claiming divine authority for what he writes. A closer acquaintance with Paul's words in these verses, however, immediately refutes this argument. What Paul in these verses is stressing is (1) the fact that, in the tradition of the words Jesus spoke while He was on earth, there are words of the Lord pertaining to certain aspects of the matter he is discussing and most naturally he gladly makes use of these words,

¹ Regarding the Johannine epistles, Harnack wrote the following words, which are of great importance for our subject: "these letters were composed by a man who, whatever he may have been, claimed and exercised apostolic authority over a large number of the Churches" (*The Expansion of Christianity in the First Three Centuries*, Eng. trans., 1904, vol. i, p. 399, n. 2). We cannot here enter upon a discussion of the authorship of the letters. But we, being convinced that they are written by the Apostle John, cannot help seeing in the above statement of Harnack another clear indication of the fact that the original apostles acted and had great influence as the שְׁלוּחִים of the Lord. Eusebius, *H.E.* iii, 23, writes of the Apostle John's stay in Patmos and Ephesus, and adds that "he used also to go when he was asked, to the neighbouring districts . . . in some places to appoint overseers, in others to reconcile whole Churches. . . ." As it seems that Eusebius based these statements on substantial evidence, we have here also a reflection of exceptional authority exercised by John.

which he accepts as absolutely final—coming as they do from the Lord of all truth and authority; and (2) he states that on other aspects of the matter Jesus did not, while He was on earth, make any explicit statements, so that Paul there gives his own commands. That in doing this he still claims to be speaking with authority follows from the fact that after he had written in 1 Corinthians vii. 12 "to the rest say I, not the Lord . . ." he proceeds to give different commands and in verse 17 declares explicitly: "And so ordain I in all the churches." In verse 25 he says: "Now concerning the virgins I have no command of the Lord", and then proceeds: "but I give my judgement, as one that obtained mercy of the Lord to be faithful." And in verse 40 he again claims that he is speaking as one "having the Spirit of God". Accordingly there are in this chapter no grounds for arguing that Paul does not claim authority for his epistles. In stating that regarding certain practical matters there are no definite words of Jesus in the tradition of the words He spoke while on earth, he is remarkably careful to stress at the same time that he is still speaking as the apostle of the Lord having the guidance of the Spirit and thus possesses not only the right, the ἐξουσία, to give instructions, but also the necessary wisdom. So this chapter also falls into wonderful harmony with the rest of the chapters of this letter in which Paul, just as in his other letters, writes as the divinely authorized apostle of Jesus the Lord and of God the Father (cf. 1 Cor. i. 1, ii. 13, iii. 10, iv. 16 f., ix. 1, 2, xi. 1, xiv. 31, xv. 8–11).

In this very letter the apostle wrote those unequivocal words: "If any man thinketh himself to be a prophet, or spiritual, let him take knowledge of the things which I write unto you, that they are the commandment of the Lord" (1 Cor. xiv. 37). Where, then, is there any sign here that Paul was merely writing ordinary Christian letters as is so often declared?[1]

And these words of Paul are no solitary words regarding this matter in his epistles. In every one of his letters it is clear that he writes as the divinely authorized ἀπόστολος of the Lord and he repeatedly states this in explicit ways. In 2 Corinthians x. 11 he says:

[1] Eg. Jülicher-Fascher, *Einl. in das N.T.*, pp. 458 ff.

"What we are by letters when we are absent, such we are also in deed when we are present." His letters are thus looked upon as an "Ersatz" (substitute) for his own presence as apostle of Christ. In 2 Thessalonians ii. 14, speaking of the Thessalonian believers, he says: "[the salvation] whereunto he called you through our gospel . . .", and in the following verse: "So then, brethren, stand fast, and hold the traditions which ye were taught, whether by word, or by epistle of ours."

Absolute authority claimed for his epistles

He thus claims the same absolute authority for his epistles as for his oral preaching and teaching. To stress this fact even more, he declares in iii. 14: "And if any man obeyeth not our word by this epistle, note that man, that ye have no company with him, to the end that he may be ashamed." Who but the especially chosen ἀπόστολος τοῦ χριστοῦ dares to write thus? To make it clear that although this particular letter is written also in the name of Silvanus and Timothy (2 Thess. i. 1) it is in full reality his authoritative epistle Paul ends the letter with the words: "The salutation of me Paul with mine own hand, which is the token in every epistle: so I write. The grace of our Lord Jesus Christ be with you all." Regarding his writing of 2 Corinthians, he declared: "In the sight of God speak we in Christ" (2 Cor. xii. 19).

Claiming to write with such an authority as seen in the different quotations from his epistles, it follows naturally that Paul gave commands such as that in 1 Thessalonians v. 27: "I adjure you by the Lord that this epistle be read to all the brethren" (cf. also Col. iv. 16).

We have clearly seen that the New Testament teaches and reveals consistently that Jesus as Lord of His Church after His return to the Father laid the foundations of His Church in a unique manner through men whom He called and equipped to be His apostles and who themselves claimed to possess and exercised the authority given to them by the Lord. Let us now enquire what the belief of the Early Church was regarding this matter.

III

THE AUTHORITY OF THE APOSTLES WAS ACKNOWLEDGED IN THE EARLY CHURCH

ALREADY in the New Testament itself there are clear indications of the fact that the authority Jesus gave to His apostles and which they themselves claimed to possess and exercised was acknowledged in the Early Church.[1] In the first place there is the evidence in the book of Acts in which it is shown how individual believers as well as the Churches as a whole honoured above all other men the apostles (the Twelve and Paul) as their leaders and accepted their authority as שְׁלוּחִים of the Lord. Compare, for instance, Acts ii. 42, where it is said of the first believers: "they continued steadfastly in the apostles' teaching..." In Acts iv. 32–5 it is stated of the believers who sold their possessions that they "brought the prices of the things that were sold, and laid them at the apostles' feet" (verses 34 f.). The same happened when Barnabas sold his field, for "he brought the money and laid it at the apostles' feet". When seven men had to be appointed as deacons they were "set before the apostles: and when they had prayed, they [the apostles] laid their hands on them" (Acts vi. 6). And when Paul after his conversion came to Jerusalem "Barnabas took him, and brought him to the apostles" (Acts ix. 26).

That Luke, the author of Acts, himself acknowledge the authority of the apostles is proved by his incorporation of so much material in his book in which the fact that the apostles were the שְׁלוּחִים of

---

[1] In the following words is a summary of one aspect of the situation in the Early Church: "All stood under the authority of the apostles to whom the Lord Himself had given the right of pronouncing the final verdict on all questions relating to the proper form of worship (Matt. xviii. 18)" (Lietzmann, *Beginnings of the Christian Church*, p. 92).

the Lord is clearly set forth. See Acts i. 2 ff., i. 15-26, ii. 14, 43, iv. 33, v. 12-16, vi. 2-6, viii. 14-24, x. 40 ff. for his acceptance of the authority of the Twelve.[1] And see ix. 1-22, xiii. 13, xvii. 13, xviii. 11, xix. 8-20, xx. 17-27, xxii. 6-21, xxvi. 12-18, xxviii. 30-1 for his witnessing to the authority of Paul. Of special significance is the fact that he three times incorporates descriptions of how Paul was called by the living Lord to become His apostle. By this he obviously wants to emphasize that Paul is just as definitely an apostle of the Lord as the original Twelve whose authority as apostles he so clearly portrayed in the first chapters of his book. From this appears the shallowness of Harnack's view that because, apart from Acts xiv. 4, 14, Luke never calls Paul explicitly an apostle "he cannot have been an apostle to Luke, except in the wider sense of the term" (*Expansion of Christianity*, i, p. 405). Of course Paul, not having been one of the Lord's disciples during His ministry, could never become one of the Twelve. But from the way in which Luke devotes so much space to reports of Paul's meeting with the risen Lord and of his call to be His witness to the Gentiles, as well as by the whole picture he draws of the pre-eminent *rôle* Paul played in those vital years, it follows naturally that Luke considered Paul to be the apostle to the Gentiles in an absolutely unique sense. Of no other Christian leader does Luke relate that the Lord in such a mighty way changed his whole life and called him to be His witness as He did with Paul. In Acts there clearly stand out as the supreme human authorities in the Church: the original Twelve and Paul.

Paul's acknowledgement of apostleship of original apostles

We have already noticed the important circumstance that Paul, although so supremely conscious of his being called as an apostle of the Lord, unhesitatingly accepted the fact of the apostleship of the original Twelve. Compare 1 Corinthians xv. 5-11. The last

[1] Note especially also how Luke, whenever he mentions the elders in the Church as also being men of importance, clearly distinguishes between them and the twelve apostles, and every time gives pre-eminence to the apostles (e.g. Acts xv. 2, 4, 6, 13).

verse is especially important in showing that Paul saw no clash between his preaching and that of the other apostles, for he declares: "Whether then it be I or they [the other apostles—verse 9] so we preach, and so ye believed." When we take further into consideration what Paul teaches concerning himself and the other apostles in 1 Corinthians xii. 28, Ephesians iii. 5 and iv. 11 we cannot but feel that the theories still clung to by men like Lietzmann[1] as to the existence of a bitter and prolonged antagonism between Paul and the original Twelve are inconsistent with the facts. It is true that Paul pointed to his ultimate independence from the original Twelve in strong terms in Galatians. But we must not forget that in this same epistle the apostle wrote the following words: "he that wrought for Peter unto the apostleship of the circumcision wrought for me also unto the Gentiles" (Gal. ii. 8). However strongly he withstood Peter when he, in a certain situation, had been untrue to his calling as an apostle of the Saviour (Gal. ii. 11), there is nowhere in the New Testament or early Christian literature any definite sign of a permanent feud between Paul and Peter. To take 1 Corinthians i. 12, as Lietzmann[2] does, as proof that Peter had been following in the footsteps of Paul in order to organize the Church (more Judaistically) against Paul is surely precarious. Paul in these verses is not casting any reflection on the deeds or attitudes of Peter or Apollos, but is reprimanding the Corinthians that they, instead of following Christ, are so fleshly-minded that, according to their different inclinations, they form themselves into parties, the one choosing him as their leader and others choosing Peter, and still others Apollos. By his words following verse 12 it becomes quite clear that what we have said here was indeed his meaning; for he says: "Is Christ divided? was Paul crucified for you? or were ye baptized into the name of Paul?" Surely, if he had heard, as Lietzmann contends, that Peter had been forming a party in opposition to him in Corinth, he would not have used these words, but would rather have asked: "was Peter or Apollos crucified for you? or were ye baptized into the name of Peter or Apollos?"

---

[1] Cf. his *Beginnings of the Christian Church*, pp. 141 ff.
[2] *Op cit.*, pp. 141 ff. and cf. also p. 200.

Instead of asking any such thing or giving any other sign that he is aiming his words against Peter, it is in this very letter that we have the words in which Paul describes how the Lord appeared to the Twelve and to Peter also separately after the resurrection (1 Cor. xv. 5), and we read that, after having called himself "the least of the apostles" (verse 9), he declares in verse 11: "Whether then it be I or they, so we preach, and so ye believed."[1] Far from showing that there was disharmony between Paul and the other apostles, this letter emphatically proves how the exalted Lord through His Spirit, notwithstanding the tremendous problems His apostles had to face, enabled them to act as His שְׁלוּחִים in remarkable harmony.

Leaving aside here the question of the authorship of 2 Peter, there is, in the light of what we have seen above, not the slightest improbability that Peter himself could have written: "And account that the longsuffering of the Lord is salvation; even as our beloved brother Paul also, according to the wisdom given to him, wrote unto you; as also in all his epistles" (2 Pet. iii. 15 f.).

All available evidence from the first century of our era within and without the New Testament shows that, apart from the solitary instance mentioned in Galatians ii. 11, the original apostles and Paul, "the apostle to the Gentiles", acknowledged and respected each other's authority as men being the שְׁלוּחִים of their Lord.[2]

[1] This at the same time proves the baselessness of Leitzmann's theories that in 2 Corinthians xi. 13–15 and Galatians ii. 4 Paul was attacking Peter and James and was calling them "false apostles" and "false brethren". It really is surprising to what extent a scholar like H. Lietzmann is still under the spell of the Baur-Tübingen hypotheses so that he overlooks all the clear evidence pointing to Paul's acknowledgement of the authority of the other apostles and of James, the brother of the Lord, and in a subjective way ascribes a totally wrong meaning to the apostle's words.

[2] H. Lietzmann declares of the epistle of James: "Here we have a definite and conscious polemic against the teaching of Paul" (*Beginnings of the Christian Church*, p. 269), thus implying that even within the inner circles of the Church a Christian believer repudiated the authority of Paul. We cannot enter here into a detailed discussion of the matter, but wish to express it as our firm conviction that there is no real factual basis for Lietzmann's statement. In final analysis, the teaching of Paul and that in the epistle of James are in complete harmony. "The discrepancies between them are purely verbal, and are readily resolved when one penetrates to the real meaning of each" (G. B. Stevens, *The Theology of the New Testament*, 2nd edn., 1931 reprint Edinburgh, 292). For a thorough discussion cf.

The true believers acknowledged the authority of the apostles

Before proceeding to the writings of the Early Church outside the New Testament we still wish to point to 2 Peter iii. 2, where the readers are urged to remember "the commandment of the Lord and Saviour through your apostles", and to Jude xvii: "But ye, beloved, remember ye the words which have been spoken before by the apostles of our Lord Jesus Christ", which also points to the acknowledgement of the authority of the apostles in the Early Church.[1] Although there were those who caused factions and were unwilling to accept the apostles as שְׁלוּחִים of the Lord (cf. Galatians and 1 Corinthians), the true believers on the whole fully acknowledged the ἐξουσία of the apostles' teaching. This appears, too, from 1 Thessalonians ii. 13, where Paul says: "And for this cause we also thank God without ceasing, that, when ye received from us the words of the message, *even the word* of God, ye accepted *it* not *as* the word of men, but, as it is in truth, the word of God, which also worketh in you that believe."

Stevens, *op. cit.*, pp. 289 ff. Paul and James undoubtedly emphasized different aspects of the Christian truth—but apart from opinions based upon subjective grounds there is no evidence in the New Testament that James did not acknowledge the apostolic authority of Paul, nor that the epistle bearing his name is aimed against the "apostle of the Gentiles". And in the light of Acts xv. and Galatians i. and ii. we can safely say that Paul and James, realizing that different tasks were given them, respected each other's position and authority. The more New Testament scholars have been investigating the available factual evidence dispassionately, the more has it become apparent that the Baur-Tübingen theories of the supposed animosity between Paul and James and Peter (as leaders of the Gentile and Judaistic types of Christian faith) are utterly untenable.

[1] The teaching of the epistle to the Hebrews regarding the apostolic authority is well summarized by Lietzmann in the following words: "Since the Son was higher than all angels, higher also than Moses, so also was His word preached by the apostles, confirmed by signs and wonders, and testified by the outpouring of the Holy Spirit, more powerful than the law proclaimed by angels and served by Moses" (*op. cit.*, p. 275) Cf. Hebrews i. 4, ii. 1-4, iii. 1-5.

Early Church authors' teaching

Turning to the writings of the apostolic and other Church Fathers of the first two centuries we find the same acknowledgement of the apostles[1] as the legitimate שְׁלוּחִים of the Lord.

Clement of Rome, mentioning Peter and Paul by name, calls the apostles "the greatest and most righteous pillars of the Church"

[1] Although in a few cases where the early Fathers speak of "apostles" they might be using the term in a wider sense than merely including the Twelve and Paul, it can safely be said that in by far the greater number of cases they think only of the original Twelve and Paul. Even Harnack admits: "while two conceptions existed side by side, the narrower was successful in making headway against its rival" (*Expansion of Christianity*, vol. i, p. 408). J. B. Lightfoot (*op cit.*, p. 96) alleges that Hermas uses the term "apostles" in a very wide sense because in *Similitudes* ix. 16 he speaks of "apostles and teachers" being forty in number. But how can we know whether he did not mean "the twelve apostles, and Paul and twenty-seven teachers"? Or if (as is probable) the number forty was meant by Barnabas to be taken symbolically, why can his expression not be taken as meaning "the perfect number of apostles (the Twelve and Paul) and their helpers, the teachers"? Cf. *infra* for other words of Hermas concerning the fundamental importance of the original apostles.

It is true that Ireneaus, Tertullian, Origen and other later Church Fathers sometimes spoke of the Seventy and of other early believers as "apostles". But there can be no doubt that all the most important Church authors of the first, second and third centuries looked upon the apostleship of the Twelve and of Paul as of supreme and unique character. Only in the wider sense of the term did they apply it to others in order to point to these early leaders as also important "missionaries" (people sent by the Churches with commission and authority), without, however, placing them on the same plane as the Twelve and Paul. In Luke x. 1 the verb ἀποστέλλειν is used of the sending of the Seventy, so that they are in the wider sense also "apostles". But, as Luke shows clearly in the Gospel and in Acts, only the Twelve are in the supreme sense the "apostles of the Lord" through whom He laid the foundations of the Church, and Paul is "the apostle to the Gentiles called and appointed by the living Lord Himself". Luke does not explicitly call Paul "the apostle of the Lord". Only in Acts xiv. 4, 14 does he apply the term "apostle" to him in conjunction with Barnabas, and then only in the wider sense—they being missionaries sent by the Church at Antioch. By the way in which he in no less than three places in Acts incorporates the reports of Paul's conversion and of his commission by the Lord Himself and by the prominent place he gives to him in the whole of Acts, Luke, however, clearly shows that Paul was in a unique sense the "apostle of the Lord, sent to the Gentiles". So Luke leaves no room for doubt that the Twelve and Paul are in the highest sense of the word the only שְׁלוּחִים of the Lord.

(*To the Corinthians*, par. 5). And in par. 42 he shows clearly that he realized that they were the finally authoritative ἀπόστολοι τοῦ κυρίου by declaring: "The apostles received the gospel for us from the Lord Jesus Christ; Jesus Christ was sent forth from God. So then Christ is from God, and the apostles are from Christ. Both therefore came of the will of God in the appointed order. Having therefore received a charge, and having been fully assured through the resurrection of our Lord Jesus Christ and confirmed in the word of God with full assurance of the Holy Ghost, they went forth with the glad tidings that the kingdom of God should come. So preaching everywhere in country and town, they appointed their first-fruits, when they had proved them by the Spirit, to be overseers and deacons unto them that should believe."

Clement could surely not have made it clearer that he (and therefore also the Church in Rome, as he is writing in their name) fully acknowledges that the apostles[1] had the ἐξουσία both to teach and to act (to proclaim the Gospel and to regulate the life of the Church) in the name of the Lord as His שְׁלוּחִים.

In par. 44 Clement says the apostles[2] even received complete foreknowledge regarding certain matters through the Lord Jesus Christ. Then there are those important words of his in par. 47: "Take up the epistle of the blessed Paul[3] the apostle (ἀπόστολος). What wrote he first unto you in the beginning of the Gospel? Of a truth he charged you in the Spirit concerning himself and Cephas

---

[1] Even Harnack, who tries so hard to prove that the Early Church was confused as to who really were to be reckoned as apostles, admits: "That the epistle of Clement uses 'apostles' merely to denote the original apostles and Paul, is perfectly clear" (*Expansion of Christianity*, i. p. 406).

[2] Zahn also declares that although "apostle" was sometimes used in a wider sense in the Early Church as in the New Testament "so war er doch zugleich eine Sonderbezeichnung der von Christus unmittelbar zu diesem Beruf erwählten und von ihm so benannten Männer" (it was at the same time a special designation of the men chosen by Christ immediately for this vocation and called thus by Him) (*Geschichte des N.T. Kanon*, i, p. 805). Paul was, of course, also included (*ibid*., pp. 807 f.).

[3] "Clement already not only quotes St. Paul as authoritative, but models his thoughts and language on St. Paul's in a way which shows his perfect familiarity with the apostle's words" (H.M. Gwatkin, *Early Church History*, 2nd edn., London, 1912, reprint 1927, Vol. I, p. 282).

and Apollos, because that even then ye had made parties. Yet that making of parties brought less sin upon you; for ye were partisans of apostles that were highly reputed, and of a man approved in their sight."

Significant conclusion

A number of significant conclusions can be drawn from these words: (1) they show that the letter of Paul referred to was well known at least in Rome and in Corinth and that it was looked upon as clothed with the authority of an ἀπόστολος (Clement calls Paul here explicitly ἀπόστολος); (2) the epistle was looked upon as so authoritative that it is called "the Gospel" (by this Clement surely means that the epistle, being one of Paul's, the שָׁלִיחַ of the Lord, is an authoritative part of the Gospel, the κηρυγμα concerning Jesus, as it was given to the Church by God through the apostles); (3) he further shows that he realized what the true nature of an apostle was by clearly setting Peter and Paul as apostles in a class of their own while describing Apollos as merely "a man approved in their sight".

Taking all the evidence of this letter of the Church of Rome[1] (through Clement) to the Church of Corinth (par. 1) into consideration, it becomes clear that the apostles at the end of the first century were still, just as in the earliest days of the Church, acknowledged as the legitimate שְׁלוּחִים of the Lord and that their oral as well as written teachings were accepted as finally authoritative.[2]

[1] Although the letter itself is claimed to be written "by us through the Holy Spirit" (par. 63), it nowhere claims to possess the type of final authority it ascribes to the apostles and their writings. The Church at Rome looked upon herself as called and inspired by God to entreat the Corinthians to restore the unity in their disrupted Church, and while doing this points to the absolute authority of the apostles of the Lord—trying to persuade the schismatics to be united with the other believers on the basis of truth and Christian life as taught and exemplified by the apostles. There is therefore no evidence in the letter that Clement, as mouthpiece of the Church at Rome, claimed apostolic authority.

[2] For the Early Church the apostles were "nicht nur geschichtliche Grözen der Vergangenheit; sie sind Auktoritäten für die Gegenwart und alle Zukunft der Kirche" (not merely historically important persons of the past; they are authorities for the present and for the whole future of the Church) (*Zahn, Geschichte des N.T. Kanon*, i, p. 808).

The statement made by Jülicher-Fascher[1] that Paul claimed no more authority for his letters than did a second-century author like Ignatius is, apart from all the other facts we have already mentioned to show its untenableness, proved to be off the mark by words of Ignatius such as: "I do not command you, as though I were somewhat. For even though I am in bonds for the Name's sake, I am not yet perfected in Jesus Christ. (For) now am I beginning to be a disciple; and I speak to you as to my school-fellows. For I ought to be trained by you. . . ." (*To the Ephesians*, par. 3). Can we imagine the Apostle Paul writing thus?

Whereas Ignatius here acknowledged his own imperfection, a few paragraphs later he writes of Paul as he "who was sanctified, who obtained a good report, who is worthy of all felicitation; in whose footsteps I would fain be found treading, when I shall attain unto God; who in every letter maketh mention of you in Christ Jesus" (*idem*, par. 12). So here we again have the clear acknowledgement of the fundamental importance of the apostle, and also of the fact that his epistles were widely known and honoured.

That Ignatius did not restrict his acknowledgement of apostolic authority to Paul appears from his words in his letter to the Magnesians where (par. 6) he speaks of "the council of the apostles"[2] in such a way as to emphasize their supreme authority. And in par. 7 he says: "the Lord did nothing without the Father (being united with Him), either by Himself or by the apostles." Add to this his words in par. 13: "Do your diligence therefore that ye be confirmed in the ordinances of the Lord and of the apostles", and we see clearly how he, too, accepted the apostles as the ἀπόστολοι τοῦ κυρίου through whom the Lord laid the foundations of the Church once and for all. And that he accepted the apostolic writings known

[1] *Einl. in das N.T.*, pp. 458 f.
[2] Even Harnack has to declare that "In the dozen passages where the word 'apostle' occurs in Ignatius there is not a single one which renders it probable that the word is used in its wider sense. On the contrary, there are several in which the only possible allusion is to the primitive apostles. We must therefore conclude that by 'apostle' Ignatius simply and solely understood the Twelve and Paul" (*Expansion of Christianity*, i, p. 408). In note 2 on the same page he declares: "During the course of the second century it became more rare than ever to still confer the title of 'apostle' on any except the biblical apostles."

to him as authoritative follows from his words in the letter to the Ephesians, par. 12, compared with par. 13 of that to the Magnesians, the introductory paragraph and par. 3 in his letter to the Trallians, and par. 4 in his letter to the Romans. That he presupposes a general knowledge of Paul's epistles appears from his words, "which Church also I salute in the divine plenitude after the apostolic fashion" (*Trallians*, introd. par.).

Ignatius' acknowledgement of the supreme authority given by the Lord to His apostles appears further in the following words: "I did not think myself competent for this, that being a convict I should order you as though I were an apostle" (*Trallians*, i. par.3). In his epistle to the Romans, par. 4, he says the same still more explicitly: "I do not enjoin you, as Peter or Paul did. They were apostles, I am a convict." (Does his explicit mention of Peter and Paul and his speaking of his letters show that he knew letters both of Peter and of Paul?)

Accepted as canonical

That Ignatius accepted the apostles not merely as authoritative but as authoritative in the highest[1] sense, and thus as canonical, can probably be concluded from his statement in *Philadelphians*, par. 5: "But your prayer will make me perfect (unto God), that I may

[1] Cf. Jülicher-Fascher's statement that the Ignatian letters appeal to the apostles "als unumstöszliche Autorität" (as incontrovertible authority) (*op. cit.*, p. 464). In the light of the evidence we find in the New Testament and in the apostolic writings, we, however, radically disagree with Jülicher-Fascher's statement (*ibid.*, p. 465) that it was only about A.D. 150 that the authority of the apostles was transferred to their writings. From earliest times the apostolic writings were looked upon as just as authoritative as their oral teachings (*vide infra et supra*). To a certain extent it is true that in the Early Church it was asked whether books are "erbaulich und der Gemeinde nützlich" (edifying and useful to the congregation) (*ibid.*, p. 468). But by far the most potent factor which led to the general acceptance of the books of the New Testament was the fact that they were accepted as clothed (directly or indirectly) with the supreme authority of the apostles of the Lord. Other factors were of secondary importance. As we see more and more what fundamental authority the apostles received and exercised and how the Early Church acknowledged it, we are more and more driven to the conclusion that it was above all through the medium of His apostles that the Lord gave to His Church not only the original proclamation of the Gospel but also the written New Testament.

attain unto the inheritance wherein I have found mercy, taking refuge in the Gospel . . . and in the apostles. . . . Yea, and we love the prophets also, because they, too, pointed to the Gospel in their preaching and set their hope on Him and awaited Him." He thus places the Gospel (the history and teachings of Jesus as the glad tidings from God in oral and probably also in written form), the apostles (their oral and written teachings) and the prophets (the canonical Old Testament Scriptures) on the same level. So in practical reality we have here already the threefold canonical authority—the Lord (or the Gospel), the apostles, and the Old Testament.

That Ignatius was not alone in giving expression to this is shown by the words of Polycarp in his letter to the Philippians, written only a short while (probably a few months) after Ignatius: "Let us therefore so serve Him (Jesus) with fear and all reverence, as He Himself gave commandment and the apostles who preached[1] the Gospel to us and the prophets who proclaimed beforehand the coming of our Lord" (par. 6). Here we again have the threefold authority—the Lord, the apostles[2] and the Old Testament. And that Polycarp meant also the written commandments of the apostles (and not merely oral traditions of their teachings) follows from what he stated in par. 3: "For neither am I, nor is any other like unto me, able to follow the wisdom of the blessed and glorious Paul, who when he came among you taught face to face with the men of that day the word which concerneth truth carefully and surely, who also, when he was absent, wrote a letter unto you, into the which, if ye look diligently, ye shall be able to be built up unto the faith

---

[1] Irenaeus says of Polycarp: "he was not only instructed by apostles and conversed with many who had seen the Lord but was also appointed overseer by apostles in Asia in the Church in Smyrna. We also saw him in our childhood, for he lived a long time and in extreme old age passed from life, a splendid and glorious martyr, having always taught the things which he had learned from the apostles . . . proclaiming that he had received this one and sole truth from the apostles" (*Adv. Haer.* iii, 3, 4). All this points, too, to the fact that Polycarp looked upon the apostles as men clothed with highest authority by the Lord.

[2] Having had to admit that Ignatius meant by "apostles" only the Twelve and Paul, Harnack says of Justin in this matter: "he would hardly have occupied a different position from that of Ignatius" (*Expansion of Christianity*, i, p. 408).

given to you. . . ." It is at this point important also to note how often Polycarp quotes words from different apostolic writings in this letter—according to Lightfoot: 1 Peter about eight times, Ephesians thrice, 2 Corinthians twice, Galatians four times, 1 Timothy thrice, 2 Timothy twice, 1 Corinthians four times, Romans twice, 1 John once, Philippians twice, 2 Thessalonians twice. Even if a few of these quotations came from the oral tradition of the teaching of the apostles and not directly from letters, there still remain a large number of definite quotations—enough to prove that Polycarp was steeped in the apostolic letters.[1] Thus when speaking of the apostles as in authority equal to the prophets he undoubtedly had also these writings in view. Quoting from about eleven of our canonical epistles written by apostles, it seems improbable that he could have had stored in his mind oral traditions to overbalance what he had at his disposal in all these writings. And quite probably he knew even more apostolic epistles than those from which he quotes in this short letter of his to the Philippians.

In par. 11 he quotes words from 1 Corinthians vi. 2 and expressly says of them "as Paul teached". In the following sentence he says of the Philippians that they are those among whom the blessed Paul laboured. Then there follows words from 2 Corinthians iii. 2, 2 Thessalonians i. 4 and iii. 15. After that he begins par. 12 with the words: "For I am persuaded that ye are well trained in the sacred writings, and nothing is hidden from you. . . . Only, as it is said in these scriptures, *Be ye angry and sin not*, and *Let not the sun set on your wrath*" (words occuring in Psalm iv., but also quoted by Paul in Ephesians iv. 26). Further on in this short paragraph, without ever mentioning or quoting the Old Testament, he quotes

[1] Even Harnack declares: "Die Briefe des Paulus sind frühzeitig gesammelt worden und haben eine weite Verbreitung in der ersten Hälfte des 2 Jahrhunderts erlangt" (The epistles of Paul were collected at an early date and attained to a wide distribution in the first half of the second century) (*Lehrbuch der Dogmengeschichte*, 4th edn., Tübingen, 1909, i, p. 174). And H.M. Gwatkin wrote: "The Epistles obtained a canonical position even earlier than the Gospels. They were read from the first in the public meetings like the Old Testament; and Clement already not only quotes St. Paul as authoritative but models his thoughts and language on St. Paul's in such a way as to show his perfect familiarity with the apostle's words" (*op. cit.*, i, p. 282).

from Galatians, Ephesians, 1 Timothy and Philippians. In the light of all this it therefore seems beyond dispute that by "the sacred writings" and "these scriptures" he means the authoritative apostolic epistles. So everything seems to point to the fact that at that time the authority of the apostles in practical reality was already to a great extent mediated to the Church through their writings. This is not surprising if we remember how emphatically. Paul claimed recognition of the authority of his epistles, and seventy or eighty years before the writing of the Ignatian and Polycarp letters already declared that what he as an apostle of Jesus Christ is indeed when present, he is by letters when absent (2 Cor. x. 11).

(C) The New Testament Formed and Clothed with the Authority of the Lord and of His Apostles

THE NEW TESTAMENT FORMED AND CLOTHED WITH THE AUTHORITY OF THE LORD AND OF HIS APOSTLES

JÜLICHER-FASCHER[1] wrote that late in the second century the general view was: "Die Apostel sind zwar auch, wie ehedem Jesus, gestorben, aber sie haben in ihren Schriften den Ersatz für ihre mündliche Verkündigung hinterlassen, zum Fundament und Grundpfeiler unsers Glaubens" (It is true that the apostles also died, as Jesus did formerly, but in their writings they have left behind the substitute for their oral preaching, as the foundation and main support of our faith). In the light of what we have found in the Apostolic Fathers as to the supreme[2] authority ascribed to the apostles and to their writings, we feel compelled by the sheer weight of the evidence to declare that this view was already to a large extent the accepted view of the Church of at least the beginning of the second and probably also of the last decades of the first century.

Apostolic writings of equal authority with the Old Testament

All available evidence seems clearly to point to the fact that the Early Church made much more use of the apostolic writings, looking upon them as of equal authority with the Old Testament[3] than is generally supposed.[4] When, after the time of the Apostolic Fathers, in days when the Church had to fight for her very existence against Christian Gnosticism and other movements, the appeal to the oral

[1] *Op. cit.*, p. 496.

[2] What Lietzmann states in the following words was true from earliest times (as we have seen above): "The apostles were the last and also the only (human) authorities: so ran the canonical principle which expressed the Church's belief as to the nature of her authorities" (*The Founding of the Church Universal*, p. 124).

[3] Actual evidence (*vide supra et infra*) clearly disproves the statement of Jülicher-Fascher (*op. cit.*, p. 475) that till about A.D. 150 the apostolic New Testament epistles were not looked upon as of equal authority as the Old Testament.

[4] The fact that so comparatively few "Christian" *agrapha* are to be found in the writings of the Apostolic Fathers, whereas their writings practically abound with passages which are also found in our canonical Gospels, seems also clearly

παράδοσις τῶν πρεσβυτέρων became so prominent, it is a noteworthy fact that this παράδοσις was appealed to not so much to get the contents of the Gospel of the Lord or of the apostolic teachings, but to obtain the proof of the genuineness of the contents of the books the Church had already for many years been using as authoritative, and also to obtain authoritative *interpretations* of the meaning of the contents of the canonical books. This is especially clear in the case of Papias. For he states explicitly that he will not hesitate to add what he learned from the elders, not to the "oracles" themselves but to his *interpretations* of the "oracles" of the Lord (οὐκ ὀκνήσω δέ σοι καὶ ὅσα ποτὲ παρὰ τῶν πρεσβυτέρων καλῶς ἔμαθον καὶ καλῶς ἐμνημόνευσα, συγκατάξαι ταῖς ἑρμηνείαις). (Cf. Eusebius, *H.E.* iii, 39, 1). Does this not prove that he already possessed[1] books clothed with indisputable authority (cf. his words about Mark being the careful report of what Peter preached, and Matthew as originating from the Apostle Matthew) from which he

to point to the fact that in those times the written Gospels (especially the Synoptists) played a very important *rôle*. Of the few hundred "Christian" *agrapha* Resch lists (cf. his *Agrapha: Aussercanonische Schriftfragmente*, 2nd edn., Leipzig, 1906, pp. 88–214), only twelve are from the Apostolic Fathers. And of these five are from II Clement, which does not really belong to the time of the Apostolic Fathers. So there are actually only seven in the earlier writings, and even of these seven at least some are probably not really *agrapha* (cf. Agraphon 67, of Resch, p. 88; Agraphon 68, p. 89; Agraphon 69, p. 90, etc.). As far as we can judge, there are only two cases of real "New Testament" *agrapha* in the Apostolic Fathers outside II Clement. Contrast with this the approximately eighty times passages from our Gospels appear in the Apostolic Fathers. This forcibly demonstrates the fact that the written Gospels already played a supremely important *rôle* as the authoritative proclamation of the Evangel.

[1] "Die λόγια κυριακα, die es richtig auszulegen gilt, sind da, und zwar schriftlich . . . es wird nur der Mangel an Überresten aus Papias' Werk daran die Schuld tragen dasz wir die Zahl der ihm vorliegenden Evangelienschriften nicht genau kennen. Mt. und Mk. haben sicher dazu gehört, von Lk. dürfen wir es vermuten, am liebesten aber hat er das vierte Evangelium gehabt" (The λόγια κυριακα, which it is of importance to expound correctly, are there and indeed in a written form . . . only the lack of fragments from Papias' work will bear the blame for it that we do not precisely know the number of Gospel writings that lay before him. Matthew and Mark certainly belonged to the number; of Luke we may presume this, but he liked the fourth Gospel best of all) (Jülicher-Fascher, *op. cit.*, p. 476). Cf. also E. Schwartz, *Über den Tod der Söhn Zebedai, Ein Beitrag zur Geschichte des Johannes Evangeliums* (1904), for a detailed discussion showing that Papias used at least three of our Gospels.

obtained the λογια κυριου which he now wants to interpret?[1] The information derived from the elders he therefore only wants for helping him (as already stated), not to obtain the λογια themselves but to give an exegesis of the oracles of the Lord. By his words οὐ γὰρ τὰ ἐκ τῶν βιβλίων τοσουτον με ὠφελεῖν ὑπελάμβανον ὅσον τὰ παρὰ ζώσης φωνῆς καὶ μενούσης (for taking up the things to help me not as much from the books as from the living and abiding voice) he surely does not mean to minimize the authority of the epistles of St. Paul and the other writings clothed with apostolic authority. For if this was so, why should he so emphatically have stressed the fact that Mark wrote down accurately the preaching of Peter, the chief apostle, and that he omitted nothing, nor wrote down anything wrongly? (Papias in Eusebius, iii, 39, 15). With scholars like Jülicher-Fascher,[2] Zahn,[3] Funk,[4] Grosheide,[5]

[1] (a) There is no agreement among scholars whether the λογια were only words of Jesus or the whole Gospel narrative. Clement of Rome in his *Epistle to the Corinthians*, liii. 1, seems to use λογια synonymous with "the sacred scriptures". Cf. also Romans iii. 2. It seems to us very probable that Papias meant by λογια "scriptures". His five-volumed work was entitled λογίων κυριακῶν ἐξηγησις (εις) and not τῶν λόγων τοῦ κυρίου διήγησις—a commentary (not a narrative) dealing not simply with words spoken by the Lord, but with Scriptures concerning Him (cf. H. M. Gwatkin, *Early Church History*, 2nd edn. London, 1912, reprint 1927, i, p. 282). We cannot help thinking thus that Papias' work was a commentary on the Gospel history as contained in the written Gospels.

[2] With the ζωσῆς φωνῆς, says Jülicher-Fascher, "stellt er nicht etwa feindselig aller Schrift-Autorität gegenüber . . . sondern in halbironischer Benützung eines Lieblingsausdrucks der Gnostiker spielt er seine alte, echte, einwandfrei bezeugte mündliche Tradition aus gegen ihre dunkle Geheim- und Bücherweisheit" (he does not indeed in a hostile manner oppose it to all scriptural authority . . . but by half ironically using a favourite expression of the gnostics he plays out his old, genuine, readily attested, oral tradition against their gloomy secret and bookish wisdom) (*op. cit.*, p. 476).

[3] He declares: "When Papias explains his diligent inquiry by saying that he proceeded on the assumption that he could not derive so much benefit from books as from the spoken words of living witnesses, he does not express any indifference towards books in general, which would be inconsistent with his remarks on Mark, Matthew, 1 John, 1 Peter and Revelation, nor does he say what was his own opinion of the value of books now that he himself had become an author (he writes ὑπολάμβανον, not ὑπελαβον or ὑπολαμβάνω)" (*Introduction to the New Testament*, Eng. trans., Edinburgh, 1909, ii, p. 526). Cf. also his *Geschichte des N.T. Kanons*, i, 1, Erlangen, 1888, pp. 849–70.

[4] Cf. *Patres Apostolici*, Tübingen, 1901, *i*. p. 351.

[5] *Algemene Kanoniek van het Nieuwe Testament*, Amsterdam, 1935, p. 58.

Stonehouse[1] and many others, we feel convinced that Papias aimed these words not against any of the apostolic writings[2] but against heretical writings such as possibly those of Basilides[3] and other writings which had no apostolic authority but purported to give interpretations of the Gospel history and truth. It is to be noted also that Eusebius quotes these words of Papias in a context where he is battling against heretical writings in favour of the canonical writings.

We feel convinced that, far from being a witness against the final authority of the writings of the apostles and of their followers, Papias also points to the fact not only that the apostles are the supreme human authorities in the Church but also that their authority is potent in the writings[4] written by them or by those who incorporated their preaching in their writings (as Mark did in the case of Peter's preaching). No one will question the fact that to Papias the apostles, as apostles of the Lord, were the greatest and final authorities. For even in seeking material for his exegesis[5] of

---

[1] "The Authority of the New Testament" in *The Infallible Word*, Philadelphia, 1946, pp. 126-8.

[2] Eusebius clearly taught that Papias made use of the written teachings of the apostles by speaking, for instance, of Papias' "reading of the apostolic accounts" (*H.E.* iii. 39). And he nowhere hints that he did not acknowledge their authority. Is it conceivable that one who acknowledged the supreme authority of the apostles as apostles of the Lord would not at the same time acknowledge the authority of their writings and of the writings containing their teachings in unadulterated form (as Mark, for instance, in Papias' own words, contained the Apostle Peter's preachings)?

[3] Zahn thinks that Basilides could have written his twenty-four-volumed (!) exegetical work on "the Gospel" as early as A.D. 120 or 125 (*Geschichte des N.T. Kanons*, i, pp. 763 f.).

[4] From Eusebius, *H.E.* iii, 39, 16, we know that Papias knew and accepted the Apocalypse as authoritative (cf. Maurice Jones, *The Twentieth Century New Testament*, 3rd. edn., London, 1934, p. 366). He also used as authoritative at least 1 John and 1 Peter (cf. Eusebius, *H.E.*, iii, 39). Cf. also no. x of the "Fragments of Papias" in Bishop Lightfoot's *Apostolic Fathers*, p. 532. See also Stanton, *The Gospels as Historical Documents*, 1918, vol. iii, p. 57.

[5] It is noteworthy that Papias says he inquired regarding what the apostles "said", not what they "preached" or "proclaimed". Does this not also hint at the fact that what Papias was looking for in the oral tradition was not the Lord's "oracles" themselves, but that he was eager to know what the apostles said *concerning* the oracles? If, as the facts seem clearly to show, he already possessed the oracles in a fixed, comprehensive and authoritative form in the written Gospels, this action of Papias is clearly understandable.

the oracles of the Lord he only gives credence to what comes from them. How can it therefore be imagined that he would have minimized the authority of books which he definitely knew to contain the authoritative preaching of the apostles (as Mark, for instance)? And does he not, by taking the λογια κυριακα from the written Gospels and[1] seeking in the oral tradition only information to help him with his interpretations, show that the written Gospels are so clothed with apostolic authority that they form for him a fixed and indisputable authority? All the evidence seems to point to the fact that this was really so and that Papias looked upon the apostolic writings as forming a category of their own.

Supreme authority of the teaching of the apostles acknowledged

To return once more to the authority of the teaching of the apostles as such (whether oral or written), it is important to note the first sentence of the *Didache*, which reads: ΔΙΔΑΧΗ κυρίου διὰ τῶν δώδεκα ἀποστόλων τοῖς ἔθνεσιν. For this gives vivid expression to the view generally held in the Early Church that it was pre-eminently through the apostles that the teaching of the Lord was brought to the Church. In passing we might mention that in the *Didache* where mention is made of "apostles" in par. 11 the term ἀπόστολοι is probably used in the sense of missionaries[2] of the Church and not in that of שְׁלוּחִים of the Lord, notwithstanding the command given there: "Let every apostle, when he cometh to you, be received as the Lord." This command of the high honour that is to be conferred on the so-called apostle is at the same time a reflection of the authority that the original apostles of the Lord possessed in the Church. That the author of the *Didache* could not

---

[1] (a) Even Harnack accepts it as a fact that Papias based his five-volumed work on the written Gospels and was only inquiring what the Twelve had said "apart from the Gospels" (*Origins of the New Testament*, p. 55).

[2] "There is no proof, and there is not a very high degree of probability, that the 'apostles' of the *Didache* are (even) the same kind of ministers as those who are called 'apostles' in the New Testament, although not of the number of the Twelve" (Plummer, *op. cit.*, p. 48). Harnack says of these "apostles" that they were "the regular missionaries of the Gospel" (*Expansion of Christianity*, ii, p. 410).

have meant men of equal authority with the original apostles already follows from the words in the first sentence of this writing. In any case the reference to "apostles" here, and the whole question of the date and authorship of the *Didache*, is too problematic to allow any important conclusions to be drawn from this regarding the authority of the apostles of the Lord.

That the author of the so-called *Epistle of Barnabas* did not claim apostolic authority is seen by his statement in par. 4: "But though I would fain write many things, not as a teacher, but as becometh one who loveth you not to fall short of that which we possess, I was anxious to write to you, being[1] your devoted slave. . . ." At another place in the same letter he says: "But I, not as though I were a teacher, but as one of yourselves, will show forth a few things. . . ." (par. 1). How utterly different are these statements from those of St. Paul concerning the authority with which he writes and speaks!

Having so clearly stated that he is not speaking as an apostle, he declares in par. 5: "[the Lord] chose His own apostles who were to proclaim His Gospel"—once more the acknowledgement that the apostles are the שְׁלוּחִים of the Lord. In par. 8 he states this even more emphatically by declaring that to the apostles "the Lord gave authority [$\dot{\epsilon}\xi o v \sigma i a$] over the Gospel, that they should preach it".[2]

Even in *The Shepherd of Hermas* the supreme authority of the apostles[3] is proclaimed: in *Vis.* iii, 5—by representing them

[1] Contrast the way Paul spoke of himself as the "slave of Jesus Christ, the Lord".

[2] That he accepted the canonical authority also of the apostolic writings follows already from the authority he ascribed to the apostles, and is clearly illustrated by the way in which he quotes words from Matthew xxii. 14, with the formula ὡς γέγραπται (*Ep.* iv, 14). A few sentences earlier he used the same formula when quoting from the Old Testament.

[3] Harnack says of the *Shepherd of Hermas* that it is "perfectly clear that the author had in view a wider, although apparently a definite, circle of persons, and that he consequently paid no special attention to the twelve" (*Expansion of Christianity*, i, p. 407). But not a single one of all the passages in *Hermas* in which "apostles" occur gives us the least right to declare that by "apostles" Hermas meant any wider circle than the Twelve and Paul. On the contrary, the way in which he so clearly distinguishes, for example, between "the apostles and overseers and teachers

figuratively as the first stones of the building that is being erected; in *Sim.* ix, 17—by declaring that "the Son of God was preached by the apostles"; in *Sim.* ix, 25—by speaking of the apostles as pre-eminently those who "preached unto[1] the whole world, and who taught[2] the word of the Lord in soberness and purity, and kept back no part at all for evil desire, but walked always in righteousness and truth, even as also they received the Holy Spirit".

In the so-called "Reliques of the Elders" preserved in Irenaeus, *Adv. Haer.* (cf. Lightfoot, *Apostolic Fathers*, pp. 539 ff.), we find the

---

and deacons" (*Vision*, iii, 5), "apostles and teachers" (*Sim.* ix, 15 and again in ix, 16), by the fundamental importance he ascribes to their work, and by his stressing that pre-eminently they "preached unto the whole world" (*Sim.* ix. 25), reminding us of the commission given to the original apostles and in slightly different form also to Paul (Matt. xxviii. 18; Acts ix. 15), seems clearly to point to the fact that he meant the Twelve and Paul. The reason why he does not explicitly say so would then, in the light of the pre-eminence given to these apostles in the New Testament, in I Clement, in the Ignatian letters, and in other writings of those times, be that he knew his readers were well aware of the fact that only the Twelve and Paul are in real sense the apostles of the Lord.

[1] The belief of the Church from earliest times (cf. Mark xvi. 20; Matt. xxviii. 18; I Clement, par. v) that the original apostles vigorously proclaimed the Gospel in many places is declared by Harnack to be without any real foundation. As explanation why the Church nevertheless ascribed such a comprehensive activity to the apostles, he offers the following argument: "the belief that the world was near its end produced, by a sort of inevitable process, the idea that the Gospel had by this time been preached everywhere; for the end could not come until this universal proclamation had been accomplished. On these grounds the prestige of the primitive apostles shot up to so prodigious a height that their commission to the whole world was put right into the creed". (*Expansion of Christianity*, i, p. 439). Apart, however, from the fertile imagination of Harnack, there is no factual basis for this argumentation of his. He seems to have felt it himself, because on the same page he admits: "We are no longer in a position nowadays to determine the degree of truth underlying the belief in the apostles' world-wide mission." This being the case, who has the right to say the tradition of the Early Church, incorporated, for example, in Mark xvi. 20, I Clement v, *Hermas Sim.* ix, 25, is without a foundation in real facts? Naturally, as time went on during the second and third centuries, the activity of the apostles was exaggerated. There is, however, no reason to doubt the truth of the statements made during the first century (referred to above) regarding a vigorous and prolonged activity of the primitive Twelve as apostles of the Lord.

[2] For a detailed argumentation concerning Hermas' knowledge and use of our four Gospels cf. C. Taylor, *The Witness of Hermas to the Four Gospels*, London, 1892.

SUPREME AUTHORITY 107

same pre-eminence given to the authority of the apostles. In practically every case where anything is related concerning traditions of "the elders" it is clearly stated that those responsible for the traditions had been disciples of the apostles (cf. Irenaeus, *Adv. Haer.* iv, 32, 1; v, 5, 1; v, 30, 1; v, 33, 3; v, 36, 1 and 2), or, in a few cases, disciples of the scholars of the apostles (iv, 27, 1). Compare also *The Epistle to Diognetus*, par. 11. Moreover in these "Reliques of the Elders" we have quite a number of quotations from epistles of the apostles introduced with words such as "the apostle did most clearly point out, saying...", or "to this the elder referred Paul's saying...", or "as it is said also by the apostle" (cf. Irenaeus, *Adv. Haer.* v, 36, 2; iv, 27, 1-28, 1). All this points most overwhelmingly to the fact that at least long before the last third of the second century the words of the apostles were constantly appealed[1] to as of final authority.

Even the apocryphal writers reflect authority ascribed to the apostles

At this point we must also note that so many of the apocryphal writings written during the second century reflect the fact that supreme authority was ascribed by the Early Church to the apostles. This already appears from the titles given to these books *The Epistle of the Apostles*, *The Acts of John*, *The Acts of Paul*, *The*

[1] Jülicher-Fascher has rightly stated that "Das Wort des Serapion (um 200), ' die Apostle nehmen wir an wie den Herrn' hätte 100 Jahre früher gesprochen sein können; in ihnen findet man alle Wahrheit verkörpert" (The saying of Serapion (about 200), "we accept the apostles like the Lord", could have been uttered a hundred years earlier; in them one finds all truth embodied) (*op. cit.*, p. 463). Harnack says of the time of the Apostolic Fathers concerning the Christian preaching: "Als die es vermittlenden und verbürgenden Autoritäten galten die Jünger Jesu, die (zwölf) Apostel. Auf sie führte man in gleicher Weiss Alles zurüch, was man sich aus der Geschichte Jesu erzählte, und was man von Sprüchen Jesu sich einprägte" (The disciples of Jesus, the (twelve) apostles, were reckoned as the authorities mediating and guaranteeing it. In the same way there was traced back to them everything that people told themselves out of the history of Jesus and that they impressed upon themselves of the sayings of Jesus) (*Lehrbuch der Dogmengeschichte*, i, p. 177). How the same author can hold views such as his well-known theories in which he tries to prove that the Christian traditions remained in a very fluid condition until the time of Marcion and the Montanists is incomprehensible.

108   SUPREME AUTHORITY

Revelation of Peter, *The Acts of Peter*[1] and so on. However weird most of the contents of these books are, they all agree in ascribing to the apostles a supreme authority. Even most of the Gnostic heretics, by pretending that their esoteric teachings came from the apostles, in this way do homage to the original שְׁלוּחִים of the Lord.[2] Marcion is indeed a remarkable exception in that he described the original Twelve as men misled by the Creator God. But by doing this he gives us additional proof that the apostles and their writings were looked upon as the authoritative foundations of the Church.[3] For why would he, in propagandizing his heretical views, have attacked the original apostles so radically if none of their writings were looked upon as the foundations of the orthodox Church? In addition, we must remember that although he described the original

---

[1] The following words from the so-called *Preaching of Peter* (written possibly near the middle of the second century) bring out the belief in the authority of the original Twelve very clearly: "I have chosen you twelve disciples, judging you to be worthy of me and esteeming you to be faithful apostles, sending you out into the world to preach the Gospel to all inhabitants" (cf. Harnack, *Expansion of Christianity*, i, p. 407). In the *Pistis Sophia*, chapter vii, the supreme importance ascribed to the apostles also forcibly comes to the fore (although expressed in Gnostic terms).

[2] All this shows the untenableness of Harnack's view that the supreme importance and finality attached to what was looked upon as the apostolic teachings (oral and written) was "acquired during the second century because of the Gnostic controversy" (*Origin of the New Testament*, p. 24). Cf. also his words: "From the first ages, the ages of enthusiasm onwards, every Christian writing counted as 'inspired'. . . . But now a new valuation according to the standard of apostolic-Catholic gradually won its way in the Church. . . . This change is only one symptom of the grand historical revolution from enthusiasm to ecclesiasticism, from the spirit to the letter combined with the spirit. Like prophecy in earlier days, all that was Catholic and apostolic had to be accepted as authoritative and no one could criticize it" (pp. 23 f., footnote). See Harnack's own contradiction of these ideas of his by his statement that Paul already proclaimed the supreme authority of the Twelve and of himself (*Expansion of Christianity*, i. p. 403). Cf. also his words in *Origin of the New Testament*, pp. 47 f., in which he admits that already at the end of the first century the apostles were looked upon as clothed with absolute authority.

[3] There is absolutely no proof for Jülicher-Fascher's statement that Marcion was the first to place alongside of the Gospels also epistles of Paul as canonical (*op cit.*, pp. 478 ff.). We have already seen sufficiently how from the very earliest times the apostolic epistles were acknowledged as having the same final authority as the Old Testament.

twelve apostles as misguided men and discarded much of the apostolic writings, he acknowledged the authority of the Apostle Paul, accepted the majority of his letters and even called his canon by the twofold name "the Gospel and the Apostle". In (what he called) "purifying" the epistles of Paul and the Gospel of Luke he did not attack the authority of the apostle, but said that he was removing later accretions to the original Gospel and letters of the apostle to whom the Supreme God had revealed the real truth concerning Jesus. So even Marcion[1] also gives powerful evidence to the fact that right from the beginning and throughout up to his time the apostles and their teachings (oral and written) were looked upon in the Church as a whole as clothed with the divine authority of the Lord.[2]

In Justin Martyr we find statements such as the following: "from Jerusalem there went out into the world men, twelve in number, and these illiterate, of no ability in speaking: but by the power of God they proclaimed to every race of men that they were sent by Christ to teach to all the word of God" (*First Apology*, chapter xxxi.) Could he have given clearer expression of the fact that the apostles were the שְׁלוּחִים of the Lord?

The same authority ascribed to the written teachings

And that he ascribed to their written teaching and to the writings incorporating their κηρυγμα the same authority as to their oral preaching is shown, for instance, by his words in chapter lxvii of this same *Apology*, where he declares: "And on the day called Sunday, all who live in cities or in the country gather together to one place, and the memoirs[3] [ἀπομνημονευματα] of the apostles

---

[1] H. Lietzmann has rightly declared that "Marcion set on one side the Biblical canon which had hitherto been recognized by Christendom, and replaced it with a new one" (*Beginnings of the Christian Church*, p. 343).

[2] For a detailed discussion of Marcion and the New Testament cf. Zahn, *Geschichte des N.T. Kanons*, i, pp. 585 ff.

[3] "Das Evangelium, sofern es aufgezeichnet ist, wird citiert als τὰ ἀπομνημονεύματα των ἀποστόλων (Justin, Tatian)" (Harnack, *Lehrbuch der Dogmengeschichte*, i, p. 179). The expression points to the fact that the Gospels are based on what the apostles actually saw and experienced, and that they were written either by apostles

or the writings of the prophets are read", thus clearly putting the apostolic writings on the same level as the Old Testament scriptures.

In his *Dialogue with Trypho*, chapter ix, 2, he speaks of the apostolic teachings as follows: "I shall prove to you as you stand here that we have not believed empty fables, or words without any foundation, but words filled with the Spirit of God[1], and big with power, and flourishing with grace."[2] Could he have given clearer expression of the absolute authority of the apostolic teaching? That Justin had in mind primarily the apostolic writings follows, for instance, from the fact that in ix, 1, a few lines before these words, he spoke of the revelation of God of Old Testament times in its written form, and also from the way Trypho replied to Justin in x, 2, where he says: "I am aware that your precepts in the so-called Gospel are so wonderful and so great, that I suspect no one can keep them; for I have carefully read them." These words of Trypho stating that he carefully read the precepts in the "so-called Gospel" surely shed much light on the fact that the Fathers of the second century meant by "the Gospel" not merely oral traditions but, so it seems to me, pre-eminently, written books.

---

themselves or by their intimate followers (cf. Jülicher-Fascher, *op. cit.*, p. 473). Martin Dibelius says in this connection: "When in the second century Justin calls the Gospels 'Memoirs' he is passing no literary judgement, for literary memoirs present us with much more cultivated and a more independently modelled kind of writing than we meet in the Gospels. . . . Justin only meant to give educated readers a graphic idea of the content and significance, but not the literary form, of the Gospels when he took the expression 'Memoirs' from the world of culture and applied it to the writings of the Christians. As a category the Gospels are something new and independent in literature" (*A Fresh Approach to the New Testament and Early Christian Literature*, Scribners, New York, 1936, p. 57).

[1] Harnack says of the conditions in the second half of the second century: "The Holy Spirit and the apostles become correlative conceptions, with the consequence that the Scriptures of the New Testament were indifferently regarded as composed by the Holy Spirit or the apostles" (*Origin of the New Testament*, p. 49, footnote). As we have seen, this view that the apostles were fully equipped by the Holy Ghost to proclaim the Gospel in a perfect way and to lay the foundations of the Church was already held by the New Testament writers themselves and was clearly taught by the Apostolic Fathers (cf., for example, I Clement, par. 42).

[2] That Justin was not speaking of the Old Testament here is clear from the whole context and follows already from the fact that Trypho, the Jew, with whom he argues, believed in the divine inspiration of the Old Testament as much as Justin did, so that it was not necessary for him to prove it.

(Although between the words of Justin in ix, 2 and Trypho's reply in x, 2 there was a break, Trypho's words clearly refer to those of Justin concerning the words of the Christian Gospel being "filled with the Spirit of God, and big with power, and flourishing with grace" (ix, 2). Cf. Trypho's words "so wonderful and so great".)

In the same *Dialogue with Trypho*, chapter cxix (near the end), Justin uses these important words: "For as he [Abraham] believed the voice of God, and it was imputed to him for righteousness, in like manner we, having believed God's voice spoken by the apostles of Christ, and promulgated to us by the prophets [designation of Old Testament], have renounced even to death all the things of the world." Thus again we see the Old Testament and the apostles placed on the same level and the explicit statement that it is God's voice speaking through both. And can anyone, in the light of what we have already found in Justin, doubt that he is here referring primarily to the apostolic writings?[1]

Clearer expression given to a longstanding belief

In the time of Justin, Church leaders were beginning to give clear theological and philosophical expression to what the Church had already been believing for many years (as evidenced by the New Testament, the Apostolic Fathers, etc., *vide supra*). But in the time of Irenaeus, to whom we now turn, the needs of the times had brought these discussions much more to the fore, so that what had been partly still latent all the years is now more explicitly stated in clear terms. But what is especially noticeable is that Irenaeus[2] and his contemporaries make these statements in such

[1] Jülicher-Fascher declares that where Justin is speaking of τὰ ἡμέτερα συγγράμματα he is including the Old Testament as well as the Christian writings in which the authentic report of the Christian faith is incorporated (*op. cit.*, p. 473). Among these writings Justin gives special pre-eminence to the apostolic ἀπομνημονεύματα (a word which points to the fact that the books contain the reports of actual eye-witnesses), and because he believed that the apostles were equipped with the Holy Ghost "steht ihm die Glaubwürdigkeit ihrer Berichte auszer Frage" (the authenticity of their reports is to him unquestionable) (*ibid.*).

[2] H. M. Gwatkin makes the apt remark that "what is an axiom to Irenaeus cannot be an erratic belief of his own. It must reflect the teaching of his master Polycarp, and the general teaching of the Churches for a long time before the date of writing." (*op. cit.*, i, p. 282).

a way as to show they presuppose a longstanding belief on the part of their readers in what they give expression to. There is no sign whatsoever that they felt that their views were innovations or that they made certain discoveries of truths that had previously been unknown. From beginning to end they take it for granted that their readers realize that what they declare is in full accord with what has been the accepted belief in the Church from earliest times. In *Adv. Haer.* i, 10, 1 and 2 Irenaeus[1] declares: "The Church,

[1] The following words of Irenaeus written to Florinus give a vivid picture of how intimate his contacts had been with men who had known personally at least some of the original apostles. "For while I was still a boy I knew you in lower Asia in Polycarp's house when you were a man of rank in the royal hall and endeavouring to stand well with him. I remember the events of those days more clearly than those which happened recently, for what we learn as children grows up with the soul and is united to it, so that I can speak even of the place in which the blessed Polycarp sat and disputed, how he came in and went out, the character of his life, the appearance of his body, the discourses which he made to the people, how he reported his intercourse with John and with the others who had seen the Lord, how he remembered their words, and what were the things concerning the Lord which he had heard from them, and about their miracles, and about their teaching, and how Polycarp had received them from the eye-witnesses of the word of life, and reported all things in agreement with the Scriptures. I listened eagerly even then to these things through the mercy of God which was given me" (quoted by Eusebius, *H.E.* v, 20, 5–8). By "Scriptures" Irenaeus obviously meant the writings clothed with apostolic authority. This statement of his shows once more how in those early days the oral and the written traditions continued side by side. But from his words "reported all things in agreement with the Scriptures" the impression is gained that the written tradition was already the primary, fixed and authoritative norm.

A little further on in this same letter Irenaeus speaks of Polycarp as "that blessed *and apostolic* presbyter" because of his direct contact with original apostles. There is no reason to doubt the correctness of Irenaeus' statements. We know Polycarp died in extreme old age in about A.D. 156. At his martyrdom he declared that he had been serving the Lord for eighty-six years. If by this he meant that he had consciously been a believer for so many years, his actual age must be taken as at least ninety. This will then mean that he was born about A.D. 66 and that during his youth he could easily have come into personal contact with some of the original apostles, for there is no reason to think that, because Peter and Paul died before A.D. 70, all the others were also dead by that time. There is abundant proof that at least John, the apostle, lived for many years after A.D. 70. (See Eusebius, *Chronicon* (Syncell. 655, 14), for Olymp. 220, incorporated by J. B. Lightfoot, *Apostolic Fathers*, p. 515. See also Eusebius, *H.E.* v, 24, 16; iii, 33, and especially Irenaeus, *Adv. Haer.* iii, 3, 4. Cf. also Eusebius *H.E.* 23, 3 and 6; Clemens of Alex., *De divite servando*, xlii; Tertul., *De Praescr. Haer.* xxxvi; Irenaeus, *Adv. Haer.* ii. 22, 5 (especially important).)

although scattered over the whole world even to its extremities, received from the apostles[1] and their disciples the faith in one God, the Father Almighty . . . and in one Christ Jesus, the Son of God, . . . and in the Holy Ghost. . . . The Kerygma and this faith the Church, although scattered over the whole world, diligently observes." In iii, 3, 4 he says of the apostolic teachings that they "alone are true", and in iii, 4, 1 he declares: "the apostles have brought fully and completely all the truth to her [the Church], lodging it with her as with a rich bank, so that any one who wishes may draw from her the draught of life."[2]

So we see how clearly he gives expression to the fact that the Lord once and for all gave the truth concerning Him, and so the Gospel in its fullest sense, to the Church through His apostles. Now the view is sometimes expressed that Irenaeus in his fight against the the heretics created this theory concerning the fundamental canonical significance of the apostles. Far from this being the case, however, in the light of the evidence we have seen previously, he was reiterating what had been taught throughout (in clearer or less clear manner) from New Testament days onwards up to his own times.

Absolute authority ascribed to apostolic writings

That Irenaeus had the apostolic writings in view when speaking of the fundamental significance of the apostles, very few, if any, will deny. We nevertheless wish to bring forward a number of his statements in this respect. In *Adv. Haer.* i, 3, 6 he speaks of "the writings of the evangelists and the apostles" and of "the law and the prophets", and then designates all by the term "Scripture". Two paragraphs earlier (i, 3, 4), after quoting from a number of Paul's epistles, he speaks of "these and like passages to be found in Scripture". In iii, 17, 4 he has the words "the apostles confess, and

---

[1] In iii, 17, 4 he wrote the words: "as the Lord doth testify, as the apostles confess, and as the prophets announce"—showing that the Old Testament and the apostles are equally authoritative, and in accord with what the Lord Himself "testifies".

[2] (*a*) Cf. also *Adv. Haer.* iii, 9, 1.

as the prophets announce", giving, practically speaking, expression to the idea of "an Old and a New Testament".

What he taught concerning the absolute canonical authority of the apostolic writings (those written by the apostles or by their intimate followers who incorporated what the apostles taught) in the passages already referred to, he brings out more clearly and comprehensively in those famous words of his in *Adv. Haer.* iii, 1, 1 and 2: "We have learned from none others the plan of our salvation, than from those from whom the gospel has come down to us, which they did at one time proclaim in public, and, at a later period, by the will of God handed down to us in the Scriptures, to be the ground and pillar of our faith. For it is unlawful to assert that they preached before they possessed 'perfect knowledge', as some do even venture to say, boasting themselves as improvers of the apostles. For, after our Lord rose from the dead, [the apostles] were invested with power from on high when the Holy Spirit came down [upon them], were filled from all [His gifts], and had perfect knowledge; they departed to the ends of the earth, preaching the glad tidings of the good things [sent] from God to us, and proclaiming the peace of heaven to men, who indeed do all equally and individually possess the gospel of God. Matthew also issued a written gospel among the Hebrews in their own dialect, while Peter and Paul were preaching at Rome, and laying the foundations of the Church. After their departure, Mark, the disciple and interpreter of Peter, did also hand down to us in writing what had been preached by Peter. Luke also, the companion of Paul, recorded in a book the gospel preached by him. Afterwards, John, the disciple of the Lord, who also had leaned upon His breast, did himself publish a gospel during his residence at Ephesus in Asia. These have all declared to us that there is one God, Creator of heaven and earth, announced by the law and the prophets, and one Christ, the Son of God. If any do not agree with these truths, he despises the companions of the Lord; nay more, he despises Christ himself the Lord; yea, he despises the Father also, and stands self-condemned, resisting and opposing his own salvation, as is the case with all heretics."

Although we may not agree with Irenaeus as to the precise correctness of all his statements, this long passage is of supreme importance. For in it is summarized practically all that (as we have seen) the different Church leaders from New Testament days till Irenaeus' day believed concerning the authority of the apostles and the apostolic writings.

In the first place he emphasizes the fact that their teaching forms the only foundations of the Church and that they gave this to the Church in written form.[1] Then he stresses the fact that the apostles, as שְׁלוּחִים of the Lord, had, through the Holy Ghost, been given the perfect equipment for their task of preaching the Gospel in a final, authoritative way. Thereafter he declares that all four canonical Gospels are either written by apostles themselves[2] or have apostolic authority behind them. (Although Matthew in its present form is most probably not a translation of an Hebrew-Aramaic original by the apostle, we feel, with many New Testament scholars, that in some or other way—e.g. by incorporation of the material of an original Gospel of Matthew—it does have an intimate connection with the Apostle Matthew.) And lastly, he most forcibly emphasizes the fact that those who withstand the authority of the apostolic teachings (handed down in the Scriptures—cf. first sentence of paragraph 1) are in the final instance in conflict with the authority of the Lord and of the Father.

---

[1] Hans Lietzmann has written the following important statements regarding this subject: "The apostles were recognized in the Church as the only unconditionally legitimate vehicles of the Spirit. Everything which claimed to be the working of the Spirit was tested by their messages. In this way their writings were regarded as inspired by the Spirit, and therefore of final divine authority. They came to be regarded as equal in origin to the documents of the Old Testament, or, to speak more accurately, as a necessary complement at its side and bringing it to a completion; they also were 'Holy Scripture'. A New Testament came to stand alongside the Old Testament and it became customary to appeal to it by using the solemn words 'it is written', in a way similar to that which at an earlier date had been applied only to the Old Testament" (*The Founding of the Church Universal*, p. 127).

[2] He stresses the same fact in *Adv. Haer.* iii, 11, 9 by calling all four Gospels "the Gospels of the apostles" (cf. also iii, 5, 1).

Taught by an unbroken chain of witnesses

Accordingly an unbroken chain of witnesses from the New Testament days onwards till the time of Irenaeus prove that not only did the Lord of the Church call, equip and send forth the Twelve and Paul as His שְׁלוּחִים, but that through those first important centuries He kept at least all the acknowledged leaders among the believers fully aware of the fact that His apostles, in what they did and taught (orally and in writing) in His Name, had final authority. So the Church, practically speaking, possessed from very early times a New Testament canon very similar to what we have today. The only important difference is that they had, in addition to the written "Gospel and apostles", a rich and living oral tradition. As far as we could discover from a systematic study of the New Testament and the apostolic and other Fathers, there is, however, no evidence that more importance was attached to oral tradition than to the written teaching of the apostles (cf. our discussion of Papias' words, *supra*). The original oral tradition was so soon supplemented by written tradition that already, in his exhortation to the Thessalonians, Paul was able to place side by side on the same level the oral and the written traditions which they had received from him.[1] Between the two traditions there was in no respect any discord, and "we shall search in vain for any suggestion that one possesses a greater measure of inspiration than the other. The one and only source of the teaching was Christ; from him the stream flows, Scripture and 'tradition' are blended in one great luminous river of truth, and do not separate into divergent streams till later times. They were at first two forms of the same thing. Both together constitute the Tradition, the Canon or Rule of Faith. (The same terms κανών, regula (sc. fidei), παράδοσις, traditio, are applied to both.)"[2]

---

[1] Cf. his words in 2 Thessalonians ii. 15: "So then, brethren, stand fast, and hold the traditions which ye were taught, whether by word or by epistle of ours."

[2] Bethune-Baker, *An Introduction to the Early History of Christian Doctrine*, 5th edn., Methuen, London, 1933, p. 42.

Uncertainty came only later on and ultimately disappeared

The reason why, for example, during the first half of the second century not every local Church and every believer had all or even most of the apostolic writings at its disposal was the result of practical reasons, such as the difficulty and the expense[1] of obtaining copies of all the writings. It was not due to lack of acknowledgement of their authority. It must also be borne in mind that in the Apostolic Fathers there is very little, if any, evidence that the authors or their readers were unable to distinguish between those traditions or writings that possessed and those that lacked apostolic authority.[2] Uncertainty and errors in assigning apostolic authority to traditions or books that did not really possess it occurred only at a later date, during the middle of the second century. This must be regarded as a result mainly of the rapid expansion of the Church during the first fifty years of the second century. The Church developed so rapidly that the intimate contacts between the Churches became looser and looser, with the result that it became increasingly difficult to hand down the information concerning the authorship and authority of the different apostolic writings. And so a situation was created which resulted in some Churches or leaders making occasional mistakes in their views regarding the authenticity and canonicity of some writings by accepting a few books like *Barnabas*,

---

[1] "Schon die Armut hatte sie davor geschützt, alle möglichen christlichen Schriften für ihre Gottesdienst anzuschaffen" (Already poverty had protected it against procuring all possible Christian writings for its worship) (Jülicher-Fascher, *op. cit.*, p. 501). This is true also in particular of their acquiring copies of the apostolic New Testament writings.

[2] An interesting illustration of the fact that on the one hand writings which were looked upon as apostolic were received as authoritative, and that on the other hand the Church leaders were usually very careful to make sure that the writings really were of apostolic authority, is the following: Bishop Serapion of Antioch when he first heard of the so-called *Gospel of Peter* accepted it temporarily as authoritative because claims were put forward so strongly that it was of apostolic authority. But in order to make sure whether it was really of apostolic origin he went to Rhossos, where the book was circulating. And when his investigation brought him to the conclusion that it was of later date and of Gnostic origin, he declared it to be false and to possess no apostolic authority (cf. Eusebius, *H.E.* vi, 12).

Didache and *Clement* as authoritative and rejecting a number of apostolic writings such as some of the letters of Peter and John on the ground that they were not apostolic.

In the main, however, the greater number of apostolic writings were accepted and used[1] as authoritative through all the years. And gradually the uncertainty about the rest of the apostolic[2] writings was also removed, so that at the end of the fourth century in the vast majority of Churches the same books that we have today in the New Testament were accepted as possessing canonical authority.

[1] At least during the second half of the second century it was clear that the main lines of our canon were fixed. The four Gospels, the Acts, thirteen epistles of St. Paul, one each of Peter and John, and the Apocalypse were accepted by all but Marcion and a very few extreme men. The epistle to the Hebrews was often rejected, especially in the West, as of doubtful authorship; and in the third century the Apocalypse fell into the same condition in the East, and for the same reason. The other five epistles were more or less admitted, but scarcely received full recognition till the fourth century (H. M. Gwatkin, *op. cit.*, p. 283).

[2] H. M. Gwatkin gives a sound summary of the facts in the following: "Other books (than the canonical New Testament writings) hardly obtained a doubtful recognition. Clement indeed was publicly read like St. Paul; but nobody ever quotes him as authoritative like St. Paul. Claims advanced on behalf of other books, like Barnabas, Hermas, the *Teaching*, or the Gospel according to the Hebrews, are not very serious. They might be read for instruction, and quotations from them might be used as garnish; but I do not think any serious argument is ever rested on them as on the canonical books" (*op. cit.*, i, p. 283).

(D) Conclusion

(D)

CONCLUSION

THE EVIDENCE of the New Testament and of the early Christian writings therefore reveals the following: firstly the historical fact of the supreme authority of the Lord; secondly the fact of the unique authority given to and exercised by the chosen apostles of the Lord to lay in an ἐφαπαξ (once and for all) way the foundations of the Church; and thirdly the acknowledgement of these two facts by the Early Church and the acceptance of the apostolic writings as authoritative. The inevitable result of this was that, as we have seen, there soon came into being (through the guidance and overruling of God) a canonical New Testament clothed with the authority of the Lord and His apostles.

After this New Testament canon, almost in its full form, had been acknowledged and used as authoritative by the Church for many years, when she was challenged by the activities and claims of heretics like Marcion, and also as a result of her own rapid growth with the accompanying needs, the Church began to give more and more clearly *the reason why she had accepted* the apostolic writings as canonical. By this she was not *creating* the New Testament, but was *rendering an account* to herself and to others of the reasons why she had from earliest times been living by these canonical writings, and why she could not exchange them for the writings of the heretics. That the Church showed some signs of uncertainty and confusion regarding a small minority of the New Testament books for many years up to the fourth century (and in a few instances even till later) is, when historical circumstances are taken into consideration, quite natural (as has been shown above). The amazing fact is, however, that for by far the greater part of the New Testament a remarkable unanimity reigned from the earliest times. No one can, for instance, dispute the fact that the four Gospels, which were from earliest times accepted as either written by apostles or by their followers, and almost all the apostolic epistles we have in the New Testament were without any serious rivals through all the years.[1] No single apocryphal Gospel and no other apocryphal writings ever enjoyed such a general use as divinely authoritative scriptures as our four Gospels and the epistles of St. Paul. Neither is there, in our opinion, any reason to doubt that all the writings in the New Testament were written either by apostles of the Lord themselves or by men[2] who were in closest contact with them or with their intimate followers, and whose writings contain that which is in harmony with the teaching of and $\varkappa\eta\varrho\upsilon\gamma\mu\alpha$ (proclamation) concerning the Lord, given to the Church through His legitimate apostles.

Our study has thus brought us to the definite conclusion that by

[1] According to M. R. James, *The Apocryphal New Testament*, Oxford, 1924, p. xviii, only the following apocryphal books were looked upon seriously by some Church leaders as of canonical authority: I and II Clement, *Barnabas*, the *Revelation of Peter* and the *Shepherd of Hermas*. And even to these books were never really given the same absolute authority as that given to the apostolic writings, such as the four Gospels and the epistles of Paul, in the Church as a whole. Only individual Church leaders and individual local Churches or groups of Churches looked upon these apocryphal writings as authoritative, but not one of them enjoyed at any time general acceptance such as by far the greatest number of New Testament apostolic writings enjoyed from at least the middle of the second century.

[2] "Das N.T. galt der Kirche als eine von altesher überlieferte Sammlung von Schriften mehrerer Apostel und ihnen geistverwandter zeitgenossen, welche in ihrer Gesamtheit eine zuverlässige Urkunde der durch Christus erfolgten Offenbarung und der diese authentisch interpretirenden apostolischen Predigt darstellen, welche aber auch von vorneherein dazu bestimmt und durch Christus und den die Apostel inspirirenden Geist darauf angelegt sind, der Kirche bis ans Ende der Tage neben dem . . . A.T. als untrügliches Zeugnis der ursprünglichen Wahrheit, als Norm der öffendtlichen Lehre und als Hauptquelle der gottesdienstlichen Erbauung zu dienen" (The New Testament meant for the Church a collection of writings (handed down from ancient times) of various apostles and their congenial contemporaries, which collectively exhibit a trustworthy record of the revelation that resulted through Christ and of the apostolic preaching interpreting this authentically; which, however, also from the beginning are designed for this and, through Christ and the Spirit inspiring the apostles, make it their object to serve the Church to the end of time next to the . . . Old Testament as indubitable witness of the original truth, as norm of the public dogma and as chief source of religious edification) (Zahn, *Geschichte des N.T. Kanons*, i, pp. 451 f.).

far the greatest and most potent factor in the forming and recognition of the canonical New Testament was the authority of the Lord and of His apostles.[1]

And so it has become true in the fullest sense of the word that in the New Testament we have the unassailable Canon ("Unangreifbarer Kanon")—the Lord and his apostles—in unassailable form ("Unangreifbarer Form")—remembering always that (as the Early Church realized) all ultimate authority is possessed by and comes from the Triune God Himself. Thus in accepting the authority of the New Testament we are bowing before His authority and not to a book as such. Our Lord, in unity with the Father and the Holy Ghost, is the ultimate Canon. Our Triune God alone possesses supreme authority in heaven and on earth, for time and eternity. Therefore we accept unreservedly the authority of His Word.

[1] In the acceptance of books as canonical, says H. Lietzman, "the principle of apostolic authorship drew the deciding line" (*The Founding of the Church Universal*, London, 1938, p. 135). By "apostolic authorship" is, of course, meant "either direct or indirect apostolic authorship".

BIBLIOGRAPHY

OF THE works I consulted in writing this book I found the following important (to a greater or a lesser degree):

BAUER, D. W.: "ἀποστέλλω", "ἀπόστολος", *Grieschisch-Deutsches Wörterbuch zu den Schriften des Neuen Testaments und der übrigen urchristlichen Literatur*, 3rd edn., Berlin, 1937.

BETHUNE-BAKER, J. F.: *An Introduction to the Early History of Christian Doctrine*, 5th edn., London, 1933.

BORCHERDT, OTTO: *The Original Jesus*, English trans. by L. M. Stalker of *Der Goldgrund des Lebensbildes Jesu*, Lutterworth, London, 1944.

CREMER, H.: "ἀποστέλλω", "ἀπόστολος", *Biblisch-Theologisches Wörterbuch der Neutestamentlichen Gräzität*, 10th edn. by Julius Kögel, 1915.

DALMAN, GUSTAV: *The Words of Jesus: Considered in the Light of Post-Biblical Jewish Writings and the Aramaic Language*, English version by D. M. Kay, Edinburgh, 1909.

DENNEY, JAMES: *Jesus and the Gospel: Christianity Justified in the Mind of Christ*, New York, 1908.

"Authority", *Dictionary of Christ and the Gospels*, ed. by James Hastings.

ENSLIN, MORTON S.: *Christian Beginnings*, New York, 1938.

FOERSTER: "κυριος", *Theologisches Wörterbuch zum Neuen Testament*, ed. by G. Kittel, Stuttgart, 1938, iii., pp. 1038–56, 1080–98. ἐξουσία, ibid. ii, pp. 559 ff.

GWATKIN, H. M.: *Early Church History to 313*, 2nd edn., Macmillan, London, 1912, reprint 1927, Volume I.

"Apostle", *Dictionary of the Bible*, ed. by James Hastings.

GROSHEIDE, F. W.: *Algemeene Canoniek van het Nieuwe Testament*, Amsterdam, 1935.
HARNACK, ADOLF: *Sources of the Apostolic Canons: with an Introductory Essay on the Organization of the Early Church and the Evolution of the Reader*, trans. by John Owen, London, 1895.
The Expansion of Christianity in the First Three Centuries, trans. and ed. by James Moffat, New York, 1904, i.
Lehrbuch der Dogmengeschichte, 4th edn., Tübingen, 1909, i, ii.
The Origin of the New Testament, English trans., London, 1925.
IVERACH, JAMES: "Authority", *Encyclopaedia of Religion and Ethics*, ed. by James Hastings, New York, 1915.
JÜLICHER-FASCHER: *Einleitung in das N.T.*, 7th edn., Tübingen, 1931.
LIETZMANN, H.: *Beginnings of the Christian Church*, New York, 1937.
LIGHTFOOT, J. B.: "On the Name and Office of an Apostle", in his *Epistle to the Galatians*, London, 1865.
MACHEN, J. G.: *The Origin of Paul's Religion*, 5th issue of 1st edn., New York, 1936.
MACKENZIE, W. D.: "Jesus Christ", *Encyclopaedia of Religion and Ethics*, ed. by James Hastings, New York, 1915.
MEYER, EDUARD: *Ursprung und Anfänge des Christentums*, Berlin, 1921-3, i, ii, iii.
PATRICK, W.: "Apostles", *Dictionary of Christ and the Gospels*, ed. by James Hastings.
QUELL: "$\varkappa\acute{\upsilon}\varrho\iota o\varsigma$", *Theologisches Wörterbuch zum Neuen Testament*, ed. by G. Kittel, Stuttgart, 1938, iii, pp. 1056-80.
PLUMMER, A.: "Apostle", *Dictionary of the Apostolic Church*, ed. by James Hastings, 1916.
RAWLINSON, A. E. J.: *The New Testament Doctrine of the Christ*, 2nd impress., New York, 1929.
RENGSTORF: "$\mathring{\alpha}\pi o\sigma\tau\acute{\epsilon}\lambda\lambda\omega$", "$\mathring{\alpha}\pi\acute{o}\sigma\tau o\lambda o\varsigma$", *Theologisches Wörterbuch zum Neuen Testament*, ed. by G. Kittel, Stuttgart, 1933, i.
REES, T.: "Authority", *International Standard Bible Encyclopaedia*, Eerdmans edn., 1943, edn. by James Orr.
ZAHN, THEODOR: *Geschichte des Neutestamentlichen Kanons*, Erlangen, 1888, i.

PRIMARY SOURCES

Apart from the New Testament writings the following were used as primary sources:

The writings of the Apostolic Fathers (in J. B. Lightfoot's *The Apostolic Fathers: Revised Texts, with Short Introductions and English Translations*, 1926 reprint of 1891 edn., Macmillan, London).

The writings of the other most important Church authors of the second century up to Irenaeus (in *The Ante-Nicene Fathers*, ed. by A. Roberts and James Donaldson, American revised edn., 1885–7; *Ante-Nicene Christian Library*, ed. by A. Roberts and J. Donaldson, Edinburgh, 1868; and *Documents Illustrative of the Early Church*, ed. by B. J. Kidd, New York and London, 1933, i).

Reliable editions of the original texts (in so far as they are still extant) are found in the following: *Die Grischischen Christlichen Schriftstellen der ersten Drei Jahrhunderte:* Herausgegeben von der Kirchenväter—commission der Preussischen Akademie der Wissenschaften, Leipzig (unluckily this series is not yet completed); *Texte und Untersuchungen zur Geschichte der Altchristlichen Literatur*, ed. by O. Gebhardt, A. Harnack, C. Schmidt (1882 and 1937);

Patrum apostolicorum opera, textum ad fidem codicum et graecorum et latinarum adhibitis praestanstissimus editionis recensuerunt, O. Gebhardt, A. Harnack, Theodore Zahn, 5th edn., Leipzig, 1906.

Altchristliche Texte, C. Schmidt and W. Schubert, Berlin, 1910.

Patres Apostolici, Textum recensuit, F. X. Funk, 3rd edn., by F. Diekamp, Tübingen, 1913 (2 vols.).

INDEX

A

Abbot-Smith, 48
Agrapha, 100, 101
ἀμήν, 22
ἄγγελος, 54
Apocryphal writings, 107–9, 118, 121
Apology, 109
"Apostle", 47–56, etc.
ἀπόστολος, 47–56
Apostolic authorship, 122
Apostolic Fathers, 90–112
"Authority", 15, 16, etc.

B

Basilides, 103
Bethune-Baker, 116
Boettner, 34
Borcherdt, Otto, 26
Bousset, 31, 32

C

Canonical New Testament, 120–2
Church Fathers, 90–112
Clement of Rome, 38, 40, 78, 90, 91, 92, 96, 102, 106, 118
Clement II, 38, 41, 42, 101
Cremer-Kögel, 49, 54, 55

D

Dalman, Gustav, 19
Davidson, B., 15
Deissmann, A., 32
Demons, 27
Denny, J., 23, 25, 28, 30
Dialogue with Trypho, 41, 110, 111
Dibelius, M., 110
Didache, 104–5
Dionysius of Corinth, 42
δύναμις, 15

E

Enslin, M., 32
Epistle of Barnabas, 105
Epistle to Diognetus, 107
"Ersatz", 84
Eusebius, 42, 82, 101, 102, 103, 112, 117
ἐξουσία, 15, 16, etc.

F

Foerster, 20, 32, 33, 36
Forrest, 30
Funk, 102

G

Gnosticism, 100
Grosheide, F. W., 102
Gwatkin, H. M., 91, 96, 111, 118

H

Harnack, A., 31, 38, 46, 51, 56, 64, 68, 71, 76, 82, 90, 93, 95, 104, 107
Hermas, 40, 105, 106
Historia Ecclesiastica, 42, 82, 101–3, 112
Howard, W. F., 49, 50

I

Ignatius, 38, 40, 93–5, 97
Irenaeus, 42, 90, 95, 106, 111–13

J

James, M. R., 121
John the Baptist, 18
Jones, Maurice, 103
Jülicher-Fascher, 36, 41, 78, 83, 93, 100–2, 107, 111, 117
Justin Martyr, 41, 109–11

K

κανών, 116
κηρυξ, 54
κυριος, 18

L

Leipoldt, L., 76
Liddell and Scott, 32
Lietzmann, H., 39, 85, 87, 100, 109, 115, 122
Lightfoot, J. B., 53, 71-3, 76, 90, 103, 106, 112

M

Machen, Gresham, 32, 33
μαθηται, 54
Magnesians, 94
Manson, T. W., 23, 59, 79
Marcion, 107-9, 118
Martyrdom of Polycarp, 39
מְסָשְׁלָה, 16
Meyer, E., 32
Montanists, 107
Moulton and Milligan, 47, 51

O

Oracles, 101
Origen, 90

P

Papias, 101-3, 116
παράδοσις, 101, 116
πεμπω, 48
Philadelphians, 94
Pistis Sophia, 108
Pliny the Younger, 38
Plummer, A., 50, 54, 71, 104
Polycarp, 39, 40, 95, 97, 112
Preaching of Peter, 108
Prophets, 23

Q

Quell, 33

R

Rees, T., 22
"Reliques of the Elders", 106, 107
Rengstorf, 46-8, 51, 63, 67, 72, 74
Resch, 37, 100, 101
Resurrection, 29
רְשָׁא, 15

S

Schwartz, E., 101
Serapion, 68
שָׁלַח, 48
שְׁלוּחִים, 51-61, 68, etc.
Stanton, 103
Stevens, G. B., 88, 89
Stonehouse, Ned B., 103

T

Taylor, C., 106
Tertullian, 90
"The Lord", 31-4, etc.
The Shepherd of Hermas, 40, 105
Tilden, E. E., 22
Trallians, 94

Z

Zahn, T., 91, 92, 102, 103, 109, 121

www.ingramcontent.com/pod-product-compliance
Lightning Source LLC
Chambersburg PA
CBHW070506100426
42743CB00010B/1772